Gestalt Graphology

Self-directed Study Course

Textbook

Cover Image by Andrys Stienstra from Pixabay

Disclaimer

Fourth Edition

2010, 2015, 2025

Write
Choice
Ink
ESTABLISHED 2021

For registered students of the course

COMPLIMENTARY

Bonus Material

You will receive a link to the following:

— Ebook: *Succeeding in the Business of Handwriting Analysis*

— Videos recorded at an introductory course to the gestalt method

— Videos recorded at Vanguard conferences. A unique opportunity to learn from highly respected graphologists

— An electronic copy of this textbook

— A PDF containing all the quiz questions that you will need to earn a Certificate of Completion (this is not the same as certification)

WE'RE HERE FOR YOU

Support and Feedback

To provide feedback or ask questions, feel free to contact your instructor at sheila@sheilalowe.com

For any questions that cannot satisfactorily be answered via email, a zoom meeting may be scheduled.

Please note:

Only those registered for the formal course
may claim to be studying with Sheila Lowe.

Table of Contents

PART ONE

SPACE

PART TWO

FORM

5

PART THREE

MOVEMENT

PUTTING IT ALL TOGETHER

Introduction

This course expands on the themes introduced in my book, *Reading Between the Lines: Decoding Handwriting*, which serves as a primer for those preparing to study handwriting analysis in greater depth. It presents the foundational principles of Gestalt psychology and its application to handwriting analysis, offering an integrative approach to interpretation. Students—especially those trained in the analytic or trait-stroke approach—are often surprised by how quickly they begin to perceive the "big picture" through this perspective.

Before proceeding, it is important to emphasize that neither method—gestalt or trait-stroke—is inherently superior. Instead, each represents a distinctly different approach to handwriting analysis, and as it turns out, individual brain dominance often influences which method resonates more with a given student. Success in either method depends very much on the student. Learning the basic principles is easy enough. Accurately applying those principles to countless different handwriting samples is the challenge.

More widely practiced in the United States than Europe and other parts of the world, the trait-stroke method follows a sequential, logical, step-by-step path that tends to appeal to those with left brain dominance. In contrast, the European-based gestalt method better suits individuals who favor more conceptual, intuitive, right-brain thinking, which affords a more holistic view.

The primary objective of this course is to develop the kind of perceptual awareness, or "eye-training," that teaches students to *see* handwriting as an organic whole, rather than a collection of individual strokes, letters, or traits that need to be *assembled* into a unified whole.

In other words, using the gestalt approach to graphology, there is no need to deconstruct and reassemble a handwriting because every sample you examine

9

is already a unified expression of personality. It reveals the psychological structure of the writer all at once, offering immediate insight into the person behind the script.

Throughout much of the twentieth century, American practitioners had greater exposure to the analytical or empirical tradition, particularly through IGAS, a school that popularized a trademarked technique known as Graphoanalysis. This has sometimes been regarded by some as a more scientific approach, perhaps because it requires a large number of measurements, which the type of gestalt analysis used in Europe and Israel does not.

It is vital to note, however, that while gestalt graphology may *appear* more intuitive, it adheres to the principles of scientific inquiry. That is, if a method consistently measures what it claims to measure, it is considered to be valid. And if repeated analyses by well-trained gestalt practitioners yield similar conclusions from the same handwriting samples, the method is reliable. In that sense, gestaltists can rightfully assert that we are employing the scientific method.

Although it is valuable to understand and know how to apply certain measurement techniques, which we will briefly address, our primary focus will not be on rigid metrics, prescriptive rules, or exhaustive trait lists. Instead we will examine three overarching dimensions in handwriting: spatial arrangement, form (style), and movement.

Every analyst, regardless of method used, must train themselves to maintain an objective distance from the handwriting under examination. Without that critical distance, there is the risk of *unconscious bias* shaped by personal prejudices, expectations, needs, and values, that will cloud the interpretation.

For example, your first reaction to a handwriting sample might be, "Ugh, that's ugly." In that moment, it is essential to silence the inner critic and remind yourself: *you don't know what painful or difficult life experiences may have shaped that handwriting.*

Always remind yourself that behind every handwriting is a human being, complete with the common struggles and idiosyncrasies we all share—and some that are uniquely their own. Our task is to understand how that person coped with their personal experiences, and how your analysis might support them—perhaps in building a more satisfying life, improving a relationship, or finding a career path that suits them.

If this sounds like a lot, you're right, it is. But think back to when you first learned the alphabet. You probably couldn't imagine ever being able to actually read. You learned how to form those letters into words. And then, suddenly one day, you looked at a group of words and all at once, you knew what they said. You no longer had to sound out the syllables. In the same way, if you devote the time, patience, and focused effort it deserves, you will discover that handwriting analysis can be an immensely rewarding field. Much of the learning process in gestalt graphology hinges on those unexpected *aha!* moments—when the pieces suddenly click into place and a deeper understanding emerges.

We are not going to spend time in this course delving into the history of graphology. There are plenty of books where you can learn about the greats who came before us—Camillo Baldi, Ludwig Klages, Max Pulver, Ulrich Sonnemann and the other giants on whose shoulders we stand, including modern day industry leaders like Felix Klein and Roger Rubin.

It is my strong opinion that while it is important to study the works of these titans in our field, there is no need to limit ourselves to what was taught in the early twentieth century, as some insist we do. Times and cultures have changed over the years. In the past, printed writing was not a consideration, while today, it is commonplace. Gender has become fluid. Globalization influences and impacts all of us, and the same is true of technological advances.

In the following pages you will be exposed to my personal accumulated expertise, which spans 58 years so far. I don't claim to know it all—far from it. I still learn new things from handwriting samples and respected colleagues. Still, over those years, I have successfully analyzed many thousands of handwritings for clients and am honored to share with you that accumulated knowledge.

Happy analyzing,

Sheila Lowe

11

PART ONE
Space

Lesson One
The Gestalt Method

The method of graphology you are about to learn emerged early in the twentieth century and is based in Gestalt psychology founded by three German psychologists. When their work was interrupted by World War II and the rise of Hitler's regime, Kurt Kofka, Max Wertheimer, and Wolfgang Kohler emigrated to the United States, where they continued to develop and teach their ideas.

At the core of Gestalt theory is this statement:

> "[Gestalt is] a pattern of elements so unified as a whole that its properties cannot be derived from a simple summation of its parts."

In simpler terms, a gestalt is what you perceive when all the elements come together to form a complete, meaningful whole, where nothing feels out of place or in need of adjustment to improve it.

---

a piano keyboard is perceived as a whole, not as separate keys.

This concept has valuable applications in graphology. When examining a page of handwriting, a good gestalt is reflected in overall visual harmony. The page looks balanced; no single feature draws the eye. There are no extremes, exaggerations, crowded spacing, or disproportionately large gaps between words.

In contrast, a 'bad' gestalt may be evident in handwriting that looks awkwardly spaced, chaotic. Or, conversely, a handwriting that is crowded or static, lacking forward movement. Imbalances such as these may signal psychological tension or a lack of integration in the writer's personality.

Understanding how to evaluate the total impression of a handwriting sample is central to insightful analysis, so as we continue through the course, we will return frequently to the idea of gestalt.

Context

One of the core principles of Gestalt psychology is the importance of *context*. This means objects—or elements—are not to be interpreted in isolation, but are influenced by their surroundings.

To illustrate, consider a piece of music. Played in the key of C it will have a particular sound. Transposed to the key of A, the melody remains unchanged, but the overall quality and mood of the music changes. The subtle differences tell the listener a quite different story.

The same principle applies to handwriting analysis. *A specific stroke, letter formation or grouping of letters may carry a particular implication in one handwriting sample, but take on a different meaning in another.* The surrounding features—the spacing, slant, rhythm, pressure, and other elements—are what shape how that stroke or letter or grouping is perceived and interpreted.

This is why accurate interpretation benefits from a holistic approach. Rather than assigning a fixed personality trait to an isolated feature, the meaning of individual elements is dependent on the broader context in which they appear.

The well-trained analyst considers the handwriting sample as a complete system: the significance of any one feature depends on everything that surrounds it.

In short, understanding handwriting through the lens of Gestalt psychology means seeing the whole before you see the parts.

Especially those first trained in the trait-stroke system it may be difficult to see the handwriting as a whole picture because they look for the familiar strokes in the handwriting. In the classic book, *Drawing on the Right Side of the Brain*, Betty Edwards instructs art students to turn an object upside down

16

before drawing it. This changes the frame of reference and challenges the brain to see the object in a whole new ways: *you draw what you see, rather than what you expect to see.*

The same concept can be applied to handwriting. Turning the page upside down changes the way you see the handwriting. You will be forced see the the whole handwriting, rather than its parts. And if you hold the paper at a distance—maybe tape it on the wall and stand back a few feet—you won't see "resentment strokes," or "yieldingness strokes, etc." It may feel a little strange at first, but as with most things, practice brings familiarity.

Perception: Looking/Seeing

> ***Perception***: *the ability to interpret and give meaning, to recognize what you see. To receive stimuli from the environment and interpret it.*

Gestalt is all about perception. Thus, eye-training is a vital part of the learning process. It comes down to two basic actions:

---

1) how you see the handwriting

2) how you interpret what you see

Perception is more than merely looking at words on a page and recognizing them as handwriting. It is about mentally organizing information that is already in your memory. Or, as the *Cambridge Dictionary* puts it, *"detected by instinct or inference rather than by recognized perceptual cues."*

From our point of view, perception means to develop a particular way of seeing the handwriting. That's why it's called 'eye-training.' As you learn the basic principles and rules of gestalt graphology and commit them to memory, with sufficient practice and experience, your instincts will gradually develop. Eventually, you will view a handwriting sample and, without consciously thinking

17

about it, instinctively perceive information about the writer's personality. You will notice and understand what is not obvious to the untrained eye (perception).

Some of the following examples of perception used in psychology courses may be familiar to you.

Examples of Perceptual Changes

In Figure 1 below, what do you see? You recognize the object as a hare. You don't need to describe the shape or background. Yet, isn't it interesting that although we perceive the hare as solid object (figure) against a white background, the figure is actually made up of separate lines. Because you instantly perceived it as a whole, you don't notice the lines.

Figure 1

Figure 2 causes a perceptual shift. Do you see a vase, or do you see two faces looking at each other? If you stare at the photo long enough, the picture will appear to shift, and whichever image you saw first recedes into the background and the other comes to the forefront.

Figure 2

Figure 3

In Figure 3, depending on your perception, you will see either a young woman or an old lady. The old lady's chin is the young woman's neck. Once your eye makes the perceptual change, it's hard to see the original image.

Gestalt Rules

In the next section we will apply three more gestalt psychology rules to handwriting analysis.

18

Principles of Gestalt Psychology

Law of good form
Objects grouped together
forms of similar shape,
pattern, color seen as one

Law of similarity
Similar objects are seen
As one

Law of closure
the mind completes figures
even though not complete

Law of continuity
Lines that follow a path are
seen as belonging
together

Law of Common fate
Flock of birds
Moving dots appear to be
part of a unified whole

Law of proximity
Objects close to each
other are seen as one

Proximity

In gestalt psychology, elements that close to one another are perceived as belonging together. Remember the example of a piano—we don't see it as 88 individual keys. Similarly, in handwriting, **proximity** refers to the spatial arrangement on the page—the distance between words, lines, and margins. When the spatial arrangement is well-balanced, it creates a cohesive and harmonious whole. However, when the writing is too crowded or the words are spaced too far apart, the visual unity is disrupted, and the gestalt is weakened.

Similarity

According to gestalt principles, elements that share similar characteristics are perceived as belonging together. For instance, group of Boy Scouts standing together in uniform is perceived as a cohesive troop, rather than unrelated individuals. In handwriting, similarity refers to the **consistency** in letter forms, slant, spacing, and movement. A moderate degree of regularity (consistency) supports a strong gestalt by promoting unity and coherence. Too little

19

similarity—excessive irregularity—creates visual dissonance and disrupts the gestalt. Conversely, too much uniformity results in mechanical or constrained writing and can also weaken the overall gestalt. We'll see examples of both.

Continuity

In gestalt psychology, elements that follow a **continuous path** or move in the same direction are perceived as being part of a unified whole. For example, a flock of geese flying in formation is seen as a single V-shaped pattern, not as a collection of separate birds. When a handwriting sample maintains consistent rhythm and direction, it supports a strong gestalt, conveying easy confidence, and integration. However, abrupt breaks and frequent changes of direction interrupt the flow and fragment the visual unity, weakening the overall impression.

Figure-Ground

Another key principle of perception is the relationship between figure and ground. In any visual field, the *figure* is the element that captures attention—the focal point—while the *ground* is the background that provides context and contrast. These two components are interdependent; *one cannot exist meaningfully without the other.*

When figure and ground are in balance, perception is clear and harmonious, with neither dominating. But when this balance is disrupted, one becomes too prominent while the other recedes, leading to visual tension. In handwriting, this balance is reflected in how the written form (the figure) interacts with the white space of the paper (the ground), influencing the overall gestalt of the writing.

In the illustration do you immediately see two sets of figures bowing to each other, or do you see the black posts between them? It's a matter of perception.

20

Applying the figure-ground principle to handwriting, the blank sheet of paper serves as the ground—the white space or background—while the handwriting itself is the figure—the dark, inked shapes that stand out against it.

A well-balanced figure-ground relationship results in a visually harmonious composition, creating a good gestalt. The eye moves fluidly across the page, undistracted by extremes, such as gaping spaces between words that fragment the text, or densely packed writing that leaves no room for the white space to "breathe." When figure and ground are in balance, the page feels whole, integrated, and psychologically stable. This balance supports clarity of thought and emotional equilibrium in the writer.

Don't overthink this. *Your task is to understand the principle, not to apply rigid rules. Bottom line, you want to see whether there is good balance between the writing and the white space of the page it is written on.*

Learning to perceive the figure-ground distribution in handwriting will help you see the whole, rather than individual strokes and letters.

Following are two examples of **poor** figure-ground relationship:

The figure overtakes the ground — not enough white space

21

There is too much ground (white space), so that the figure recedes

> Just thought I'd give you another sample
> since it's been so long. Just see - last
> time we did this you told me I
> was a repressed dyke w/ sexuality issues
> to work out. At this point I wouldn't
> really care - wanting to get laid more
> by anybody is probably more the
> norm these days no matter what your
> sexual orientation. Whatever! So, have
> at it, fire away, float your boat, etc -

Below is an example of a more reasonable distribution of figure and ground.

> Hey. I'm back. Oh I've got to let you in on this - it's really
> cute, funny and just beautiful!! Lol - Aesyah was playing
> with the door. Suddenly she just dropped down to the floor
> and started "talking". I turned and looked and saw her
> having a nice conversation with her shadow!!
>
> I'm gonna do some dusting etz. Actually, I have just moved
> back into this house. Mom and Dad stayed here alone before.
> When Dad became sick, I came back. The house is really not
> my type. HA! I'm planning to do it up according to my taste.
>
> Yin and I bought an apartment about 45 mins. from
> the heart of KL. Oh by the way, sorry I forgot about this
> now where we are in Seremban, Negeri Sembilan - one of
> the states in Malaysia - about an hour or so drive to

Why does a balanced figure-ground relationship matter?

Because your immediate perception of whether figure and ground are balanced provides critical insights about the writer. A well-managed relationship between ink and paper reflects the writer's ability to plan and organize, and manage time effectively. It also suggests how they navigate social boundaries—whether they give others the space they deserve or tends to intrude. On the other hand, imbalance points to disorganization, poor planning, and/or social discomfort.

But to fully understand what you're seeing on the page, you must first grasp the larger gestalt principles of **space, form, and movement**—the 'big pictures' that shape every handwriting sample.

How do you recognize a 'good gestalt' or a 'bad gestalt'?

Once you understand the basic principles, your first impression becomes a powerful tool. If your gut reaction to a handwriting sample is that it's messy, chaotic, disorganized, or visually uncomfortable in any way, it's probably a bad gestalt. This instinctive reaction arises from an *imbalance* in one or more of the follow areas:

- **Figure-ground relationship:** *The contrast between ink and white space is either too stark or too muddled.*
- **Form:** The style of the handwriting is inconsistent, erratic, or overly mechanical.
- **Movement:** There is a lack of rhythm or coherence.

In contrast, a *good gestalt* feels balanced and integrated. The elements work together so naturally that nothing begs to be changed or "fixed." The handwriting holds together as a unified whole.

Key axiom: *a good gestalt resists changing anything to make it look 'just right.'*

The Writing Should Not Be Perfect

Why not? Because perfection is an extreme, and extremes are virtually always interpreted negatively in handwriting. Only a machine can produce true perfection, and we are humans, not machines. Here's an example of a handwriting that appears too perfect and raises a red flag. We'll explore this in more depth later.

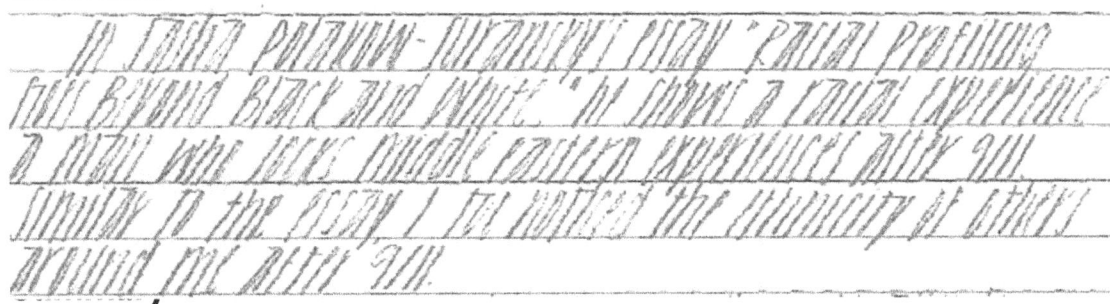

Since the nineteenth century graphologists have gathered a substantial body of empirical evidence linking specific global features of handwriting—space, form, and movement—to consistent patterns in personality and behavior. By learning and practicing the art of visual integration, you'll train your eye, and your mind, to grasp the deeper meaning behind what's written on the page.

> *To use the gestalt method of analyzing handwriting,*
> *you must first learn to **see** the writing.*

Gestalt-based handwriting analysis is neither magic nor guesswork, nor it is based on a vague impression. Like any specialized skill, it depends on a solid foundation of knowledge and disciplined observation. Mastering the gestalt method requires developing your intuition—not in a mystical or psychic sense, but as an internalized understanding built through study and experience.

In this context, intuition is the result of deeply knowing the individual elements that make up the whole, and learning to recognize what they signify about personality and real-world behavior.

24

It may sound paradoxical, but to develop a deeper, more instinctive grasp of handwriting—before you are able to truly perceive the *gestalt*—the whole— you must begin by studying its fundamental components.

These components begin with the **spatial elements** in handwriting: margins, baseline alignment, and the spacing between words, letters, and lines. In **space** we find the first building blocks that shape the gestalt and offer key insights into the writer's inner world.

In the sections ahead you'll encounter a lot of information—but take heart. With time and repetition, what may at first seem overwhelming will eventually become second nature. Gradually, your newly trained intuition will align with accurate interpretation, enabling you to assess handwriting with both insight and precision. Until then, keep this mantra in mind:

No single feature or characteristic in a handwriting means anything in isolation.

This is the essence of true gestalt analysis: *Meaning emerges only through the interplay of parts within the whole.*

Every element and characteristic must be understood in the context of the features surrounding it. One feature may serve as a red flag or a cue to look more closely—but it is never the full story.

First, you see. Then you experience. Only then do you analyze—and finally, interpret.

At the end of each lesson you will find quiz questions to help you determine whether you have accurately grasped the information in this section. You are invited to submit you responses to sheila@sheilalowe.com for feedback. Once you have successfully completed all of the quizzes you will receive a certification of completion for the course. Note, this is not a certification. If you wish to become certified, the American Handwriting Analysis Foundation offers professional examinations: www.ahafhandwriting.org

Lesson Two
Overall Spatial Arrangement

Historically, the tradition in U.S. schools was to introduce children to the basics of cursive handwriting around the third grade. In 2009, however, the Common Core Curriculum was released without any mandate to teach handwriting. This led many states to de-prioritize or eliminate handwriting instruction altogether.

The good news is, in recent years, research has highlighted the vital role that handwriting plays in early brain development, particularly in areas related to memory, literacy, and fine motor skills. A white paper on this topic published by the American Handwriting Analysis Foundation is available in a free download Click here. As a result of this research, states have begun reinstating handwriting instruction in public school curricula, and in 2025, approximately 27 states officially require handwriting to be taught. Several others have legislation pending. An informal survey suggests that only ten states currently have no specific requirements regarding handwriting instruction, but leave it up to the school districts. The question of whether these laws are enforced remains an open one.

Handwriting Training

Simply put, a child begins handwriting training by learning to form one letter at a time—this is known as *letter impulse*. As he[1] becomes familiar with the alphabet, the child moves on to combining letters into words, developing what's called *word impulse*.

With practice, the child starts linking words into phrases and sentences, progressing to *sentence impulse*.[2]

---

[1] The use of "he" as a traditional generic pronoun is meant to be inclusive of all genders.
[2] Saudek, Robert: *Experiments in Handwriting*

27

Over time, practicing leads to *graphic maturity*—the point at which the young writer no longer has to think about how to form each letter or word. Writing has become an automatic act, and there is no longer any need to consciously calculate the amount of space to leave between letters and words and lines; no longer a need to think about how to form each letter—*the act of writing has become fluid and natural.*

> **Note:** *The amount of space between letters and words isn't random—it reflects the child's personality development and emotional growth.*

The same is true in adulthood—the way the writing is arranged on the page—its spatial layout—is largely an unconscious act born of personality and behavior. Just imagine how laborious the act of writing would be if a writer had to consciously decide how much space to leave with each stroke. It would hinder communication—the very purpose of writing. Thus, unlike other elements of handwriting that may involve more deliberate control, once learned, spacing between letters, words, and lines happens automatically.

> *The spatial arrangement is the most unconscious element of handwriting.*

Let's examine some definitions of **space** that fit our area of study. Looking to how the concept of *space* functions within different contexts, we'll explore why it matters in the study of perception, handwriting, or communication.

— ***The expanse in which all objects is located.*** *For our purposes, the blank sheet of paper or other writing surface is symbolic of the writer's personal universe. The spatial arrangement on the paper offers insight into the writer's overall sense of aesthetics, personal taste, thought processes, and capacity for planning and organizing his life. It also reflects social orientation and interpersonal needs.*

— ***A measurable empty area****, often bounded between objects—such as the physical gap between elements (letters or words). This space is more than just a visual pause; it reveals how much personal space the writer feels comfortable with. The* *degree of distance between words can help answer a key psychological question: How much emotional or physical space does this person need from others?*

— *An area reserved for some particular purpose. The blank sheet of paper is reserved for the purpose of communication.*

— *A blank character in writing to separate words and enhance readability. Without this invisible yet essential "character" or interval that separates successive words in writing or printing, written communication would be confusing and difficult to decipher. Far from being nothing more than empty gaps, the spaces between words play a crucial role in ensuring clarity and readability—a fundamental component of effective communication.*

— *The interval between two points in time (or letters and words). The use of space on the page symbolizes how the writer perceives and manages time, both in daily routines and across the broader arc of his life.*

A Shift in Perspective

By shifting your perspective and viewing space as an active element in handwriting, you begin to see its true significance.

That's exactly the mindset we want to cultivate. The "negative" space ("ground") around the words is just as meaningful as the positive form of the handwriting ("figure") itself. When viewed as one, they create a complete picture of the writer's world.

Three handwriting samples follow on the next two pages. Practice observing the space *around* the words with the first sample–the handwriting of Kenneth Lay (former CEO of Enron, the company that bilked its investors out of their life savings in 2001).

Focus on the shape and arrangement of the empty spaces in the sample. At this stage, *limit your observations to description only*—do not attempt to interpret or analyze the meaning of the spatial arrangements.

Kenneth Lay

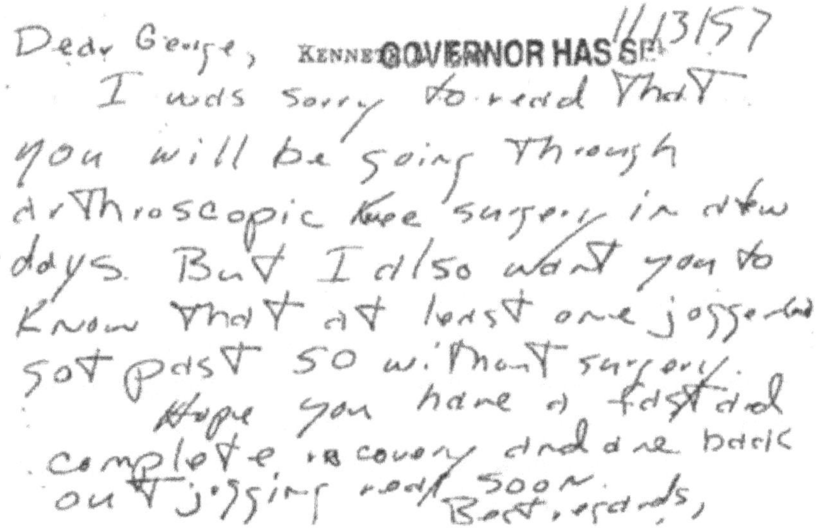

[handwritten letter, partially legible]

Dear George,   KENNE **GOVERNOR HAS S** 1/13/57
    I was sorry to read that
you will be going through
arthroscopic knee surgery in a few
days. But I also want you to
know that at least one jogger
got past 50 without surgery.
    Hope you have a fast and
complete recovery and are back
out jogging real soon.
                 Best regards,

Next, compare Lay's spatial patterns to those in the handwriting of Jack Welch (former CEO of General Electric).

Jack Welch

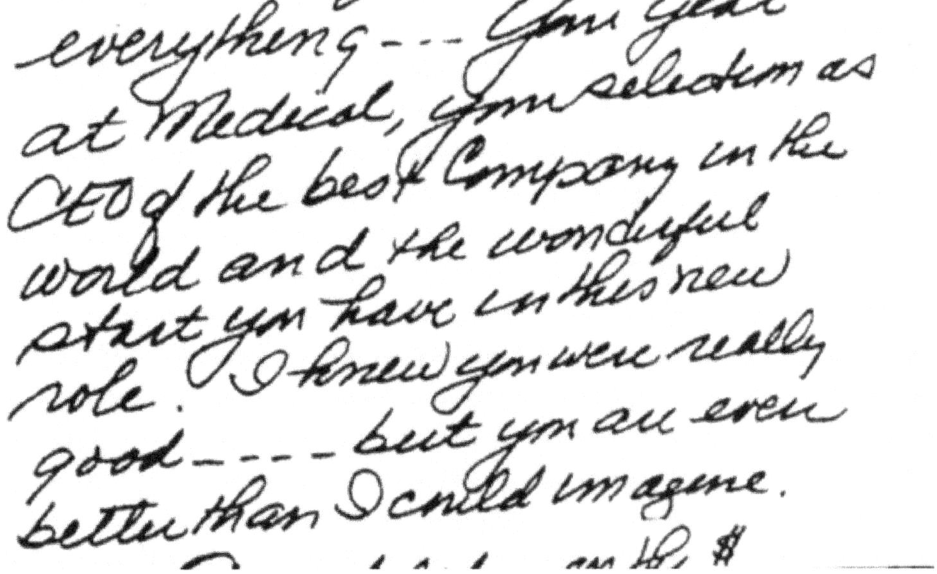

[handwritten letter]

everything --- Your year
at Medical, your selection as
CEO of the best company in the
world and the wonderful
start you have in this new
role. I knew you were really
good ---- but you are even
better than I could imagine.

Now compare Ken Lay's and Jack Welch's spatial arrangements with the sample of Dana Reeve that follows. Reeve was an activist for those with disabilities, and wife of late actor Christopher Reeve who was tragically paralyzed after an equestrian accident.

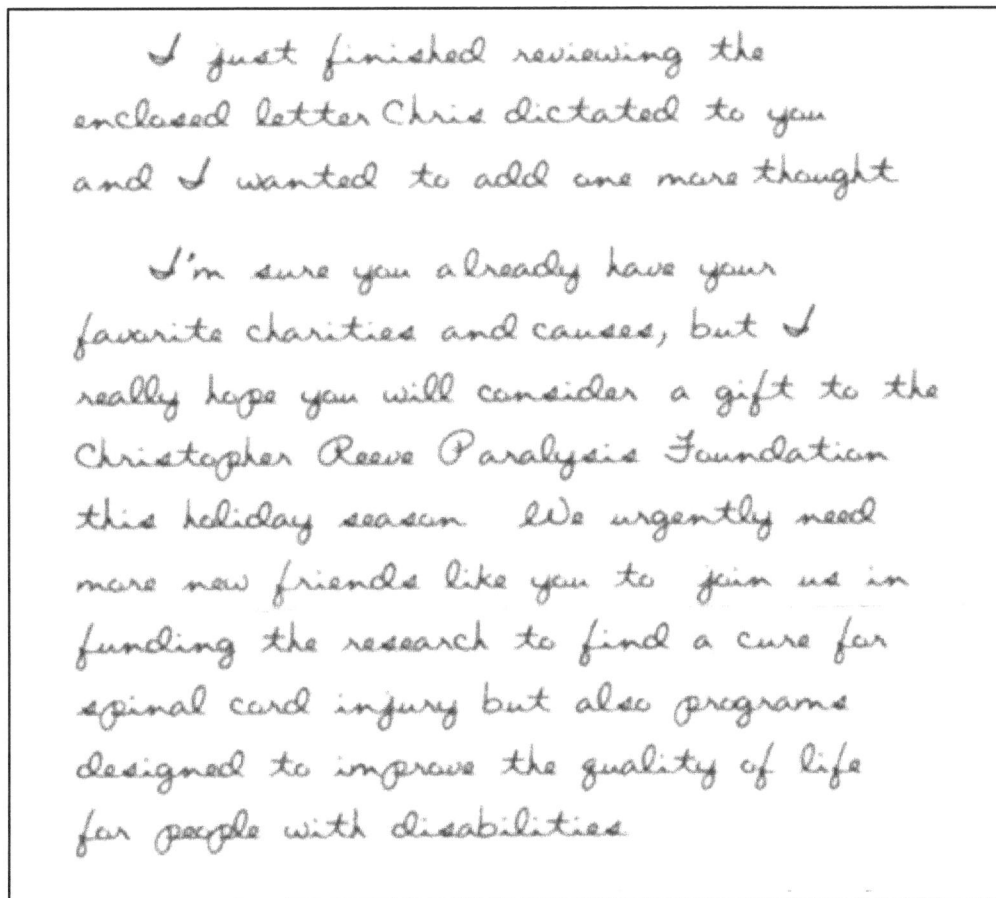

> I just finished reviewing the enclosed letter Chris dictated to you and I wanted to add one more thought
>
> I'm sure you already have your favorite charities and causes, but I really hope you will consider a gift to the Christopher Reeve Paralysis Foundation this holiday season. We urgently need more new friends like you to join us in funding the research to find a cure for spinal cord injury but also programs designed to improve the quality of life for people with disabilities

Dana Reeve

Analyzing Space

You won't always be presented with an ideal sample, and depending on circumstances may have to make do with less than you would like. To properly evaluate spatial arrangement, you'll need a sufficient amount of handwriting— preferably a full-size sheet of unlined paper (8 ½ x 11 printer paper). An experienced analyst may be able to use a smaller sheet if there is at least a good-sized paragraph—say, 20 lines and a signature.

Lined paper may be used in a pinch, but the printed lines provide a false structure and may skew the analysis. Thus, if lined paper is used, you will need to carefully assess whether the handwriting is placed on the lines, or written above or below them, and to what degree the handwriting hugs the printed baseline.

The spatial layout of handwriting falls into one of three broad categories: **Strong, Weak,** or **Disturbed**. These categories form a continuum with many subtle variations between them. Most handwriting samples won't fit neatly into a single category, and that's perfectly fine; it's not important to be exact.

What matters more than precise clarification is the **overall visual impression** of the writing. Focus on the general pictorial quality of the space; it's this intuitive snapshot that provides the most valuable insight at this stage.

- *Does the writing appear balanced?*
- *Is the writing too spaced out, or excessively cramped?*

Whether we are examining space, form, or movement in handwriting, the goal is always the same: to identify balance and harmony in the overall pattern. But what does that really mean?

The *Cambridge Dictionary* describes balance this way:

- *a state where things are of equal weight or force*
- *to give several things equal amounts of importance*

Using this definition, a handwriting with a strong spatial arrangement has:
1. Margins that measure approximately the same on all sides–they should not be perfect.
2. The space between words and lines should strike a balance—not too wide nor too cramped—and ideally, should be relatively consistent throughout the sample.
3. Some variation is good and indicates flexibility. Rigid organization on the page, which makes the writing look mechanical and artificial, is not in balance.

The next handwriting, that of Philip Garrido—convicted kidnapper and rapist of 12 year-old Jaycee Dugard—is a prime example of overly regular, mechanical, handwriting.

Extremes in any element of handwriting are virtually always evaluated as a negative.

In all respects my life has changed. Of course that is because I wanted to. knowing this is my chance to get my life in line. Drugs have been my down fall. I am so ashamed of my past. But my future is now in control.

What is 'Good' Spacing?

A helpful rule of thumb is this: the space between words should be roughly equal to the width of the letter 'm' as written in the handwriting you are analyzing. This provides a proportional guide based on the individual writer's natural letter size.

Strong (good) Space

A strong picture of space means there must be sufficient white space on the page. The Dana Reeve sample we just examined is an example of a *strong* spatial arrangement. The page looks well-balanced, like a painting in a frame. Lower loops don't hang down and impede the progress of the upper loops on the next line. The words are spaced close enough to allow a steady flow for the reader, but not so close that they crowd or touch each other. The paragraphs are clearly defined, and the margins frame the page.

A strong spatial arrangement tells us the writer has a neat, orderly approach to life, marked by a systematic mindset. Everything has its place, and each element works in harmony with others, reflecting a calm, composed, and well-integrated temperament.

The writer thrives within structured environments where routines are predictable and plans are clear. Her ability to use sound judgment and think ahead allows her to ensure that the necessary resources are in place to meet her goals. And while she values order, she also shows adaptability; when things don't go as planned, she can quickly regain her footing and stay focused on moving forward.

Weak Space

In a weak picture of space, as in the sample below, the writing is cramped, with words and lines spaced too closely together, making the writing harder to read. Although you cannot judge the margins in this sample because the full page is not displayed, in a weak picture of space they, and the spaces between lines may be uneven.

Marilyn

The Complete Idiot's Guide to Handwriting Analysis will make an excellent addition to al dready spectacular series. I cant wait to get my hands on a copy of this book.

Remember the figure-ground relationship. In weak space, there is more figure (writing) than there is ground (paper). In other words, the page will be covered with writing and you see more ink than paper.

A weak picture of space indicates one who imposes himself upon the environment. He is less interested in listening to what others have to say than getting his own point across. Depending on other factors, he may be impatient and demanding, literally filling up all space with his presence.

There is a tendency to become over-involved in the affairs of others, and a need for constant feedback. The writer does not recognize social boundaries, and intrudes on others' space. While this person may come on strong, and on the surface appears powerful, however, a basic lack of maturity in this behavior indicates that inside he feels weak and needs approval. He is more conventional than creative, and depends on a hierarchy of authority in which to operate.

The handwriting sample that we saw written by former General Electric CEO Jack Welch falls along the strong-weak continuum, leaning toward the weak side due to the crowded spacing between words and lines. The presence of seemingly balanced margins and an indented paragraph helps prevent the overall spatial picture from appearing entirely weak. (Note: the exact size of

34

the paper on which he wrote is unknown. If the writing was done on a half-size sheet, the margins may in fact be quite narrow or nonexistent). The dynamic movement and strong form saves the gestalt.

Clearly, crowded handwriting does not inhibit professional success—but it can reflect certain interpersonal tendencies. A writer may be highly effective, even forceful, but the lack of breathing room on the page can suggest social pressure, intensity, or difficulty respecting boundaries.

As always, **interpretation depends on context.** For instance, weak (crowded) space in a small handwriting may be interpreted somewhat differently than in a large one. That's why looking at the full picture—the *gestalt*—is essential.

No single element tells the whole story

Disturbed Space

The word 'disturbed' literally means to disrupt or destroy a state of calm—and that is precisely how a handwriting with disturbed space appears. It conveys a sense of agitation or unrest, lacking the peaceful, structured pattern seen in a more balanced writing.

In a disturbed picture of space, the distribution of elements is erratic and lacks cohesion. Some words may be spaced far apart, while others are more tightly packed. You might also observe zonal interference, where lower loops from one line hang down and clash with the upper loops of the line below. Margins may be extremely wide, uneven, or inconsistent throughout the page.

The greater the unevenness in the spatial arrangement, the more the writing reflects a disturbed picture of space. This lack of balance disrupts the visual harmony of the sample.

The handwriting we viewed of disgraced former Enron CEO Ken Lay has a disturbed picture of space. As the sample was written on a note card, we cannot properly judge the margins, but the distances between words and lines are highly uneven (as are other elements of the writing). .

A disturbed picture of space reflects an inner conflict—a person who seems unsure of whether he is coming or going. This writer is apt to be impulsive, easily irritated, and show little regard for the emotional needs of those around

35

him. While other elements in the handwriting might initially suggest charm or charisma, beneath the surface there may be signs of the manipulation or deceit of a con artist.

In some cases, this pattern is associated with individuals who can be highly effective in business or perhaps politics but emotionally volatile and unpredictable. Such a person might be warm and engaging one moment, then abruptly cold or hostile the next. His emotions are in constant turmoil. He may treat you like you're his best friend one minute, and ghost you the next. Consistency in behavior is lacking, and emotional instability may be a constant undercurrent.

What Are Rivers?

Be especially cautious when you see a pattern of very large spaces between words as they move down the page. This may be caused by a vision issue, which should be ruled out before drawing conclusions—this kind of spacing cant point to deeper psychological concerns. When you encounter this pattern—as highlighted below—proceed carefully in both your analysis and your assumptions.

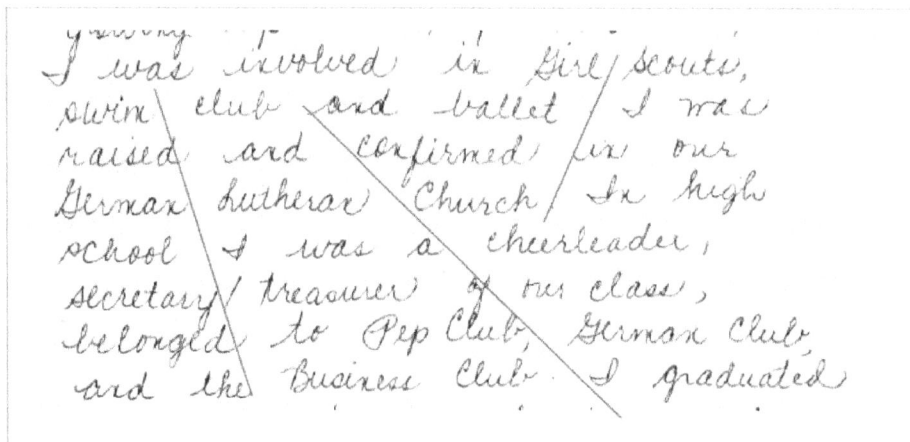

If there is no vision problem present, you may be seeing "rivers," a special aspect of spatial arrangement. This phenomenon is created when large spaces between words form a pattern as the writing moves down the page. It refers to a deep inner emotional split. The writer of the sample above killed and dismembered her abusive mother and concealed the crime for two years before law enforcement caught up with her.

36

In the End

For a handwriting to have a good gestalt in terms of spatial arrangement, there should be enough space for the writing to "breathe." There should not be huge lakes of space, nor should the page be overwhelmed with too much ink.

Balance is always the key.

When the writing form and/or movement are weak and/or disturbed, yet the writing has a strong spatial arrangement, it indicates that the writer is able to function reasonably well on a daily basis. Despite unresolved personal issues (seen in the disturbance of form and/or movement), the writer compensates for weaknesses in other areas, demonstrating by the good use of space an ability to plan and organize and execute his plans.

Lesson Three
Letter, Word, Line Spacing

Line spacing is a valuable indicator of the writer's perspective on life. Perspective refers to how one views a situation or object—and it can shift depending on one's emotional, mental or physical position. If you wanted to judge the height of a building, standing just a foot away from the wall and looking up would distort your view. You'd be too close to assess it accurately. Likewise, standing fifty miles away would place you too far to get an accurate perspective of its height and make a meaningful judgment. The same principle applies to handwriting.

Line Spacing

There is no set standard for amount of space between lines. The key is to leave enough space between lines so the lower loops don't tangle with the next line. An exception may occur when lower loops are so long that avoiding them entirely would require excessive space and would not be practical.

Note: *Line spacing depends on the overall size of the writing. A larger writing requires more space than a smaller one.*

The amount of space between lines provides a clue to how well the writer plans and organizes his time.

Clear line spacing: reflects an organized thinker who optimizes his time by planning ahead. He is mindful of his resources—time, energy, money—and tends to use them with some care. Socially, he respects boundaries and, when accompanied by balanced word spacing, is likely to communicate appropriately, both in listening and speaking.

39

I want to know how to stay on a path of self knowledge, self-awareness, and mastery. My specific goal is to be able to channel my attention and energies in /onto the path, ie, reason for my incarnation.

Wide line spacing: When the space between lines exceeds what's necessary to avoid overlapping lower loops, but stops short of being extreme, it suggests and heightened aesthetic sense. The writer values beauty, likely has refined taste, and may even lean toward extravagance, using his resources freely, without worrying about running out. Thoughtful and deliberate, he is measured in his speech, considering his words carefully before speaking.

Here is a sample for the group to analyse. I think this will be a great way for those of us learning to get some valuable advice from the many distinguished members in the group.

Extreme spaces between lines are quite rare and may point to mental illness. Extreme line spacing is wider than the **Wide** sample above. This pattern creates an imbalance between figure and ground—there is more ground (paper) than figure (writing). As a result, each line appears isolated, rather than forming part of a cohesive whole.

This kind of spacing indicates that the writer has distanced himself significantly from the environment. Rather than maintaining healthy objectivity, he

40

retreats into isolation, perhaps out of fear that engaging more fully, it might lead to serious error of judgment, or open him to rejection for not being perfect. Having backed too far away from what matters to him, the writer loses perspective on his surroundings.

*If large **line** spacing is accompanies by wide **word** spaces, the picture becomes even clearer: this is a reserved individual who may struggle to participate meaningfully in conversation, offering little of himself to others.*

Optimal line spacing shows a writer who can maintain perspective, evaluate challenges realistically, and work toward resolution. When lines are crammed too closely together, there is a lack of balance and a distorted perspective. The writer may be too immersed in daily pressures to step back and view situations objectively. Achieving clarity requires some distance—but not so much that detachment turns into disconnection.

Just as excessive distance between lines can distort perspective, **overly narrow line spacing** has the same effect. There is not enough room for self-knowledge, and the writer is uncertain and ungrounded. Though he projects confidence or even boldness to the outside world, inside he is plagued by self-doubt, constantly second-guessing his decisions and questioning his worth as a person.

Moderately narrow line spacing: the writer tends to be impulsive, often jumping into activities without fully preparing or considering what is needed for success. He may have a lot to say, but struggles to communicate his ideas clearly—especially when he feels strongly about a topic or is eager to be understood. This sample has better line spacing, but the long upper and lower extension makes it appears more crowded

The narrower the spaces between lines, the less self-aware the writer is. Constricted spacing reflects an inability or unwillingness to be open to personal thoughts and experiences.

Extremely narrow line spacing: leads to lower loops overlapping and interfering with the upper loops in the next line. This lack of separation indicates a highly subjective and impulsive outlook, in which the writer views life primarily through the lens of personal impact—how things will affect him. He tends to over-commit, immersing himself in too many activities at once. Taking multi-tasking to new heights makes it difficult to maintain structure and appropriateness.

In addition to close line spacing, then the writing slants strongly to the right, or has mixed slant, this writer typically acts on impulse without pausing to consider the potential consequences of his actions. In conversations he tends to dominate. Rather than engaging in true dialogue, he is happier speaking than listening—and does a great deal of talking.

In the following sample we see overlapping lines, known as zonal interference. The writer keeps too many balls in the air and has difficulty keeping them all where they belong.

42

Letter Spacing

Individual letters may be seen as symbolic representations of the Self. The amount of space *between* the letters serves as a measure of how much internal freedom the writer allows for self-expression. In this transition from one letter to the next—from 'me' to 'you'—we see the writer symbolically navigating interpersonal space. The key question is whether the writer respects healthy boundaries or encroaches beyond them.

When evaluating the space *between* letters, look not only at the actual distance but also how consistent the spacing is. Ideally, letter spacing should be approximately the width of the letter *n* in that particular handwriting sample.

As with all elements in handwriting, the greater the variability, the less the emotional stability, which projects inner conflict.

Average, reasonably consistent letter spacing, especially when paired with proportional-width letters, reflects an open, outgoing personality. The writer enjoys communicating and feels comfortable engaging with others, suggesting psychological balance, flexibility, spontaneity, and self-confidence. The writer knows how to give both himself and others the appropriate amount of personal and social space.

On the other hand, *narrow letters combined with wide letter spacing* creates what is known as **secondary expansion.** At a glance, the writing appears broad and at least somewhat extroverted—but a closer look tells a different story. The letters themselves are tight and compressed, while the spaces between them are artificially wide.

This contrast reveals the *extroverted introvert*—someone who presents themselves as sociable and expressive, but whose core nature is far more reserved and inward-focused. This personality is naturally introverted (narrow letters)

43

but has learned to adopt extroverted behavior when needed (wide spaces between letters).

Too-wide spaces between letters represents a kind of social intrusion into space that rightfully belongs to others. This may seem contradictory, especially since **too-narrow word spacing** is also considered an invasion of personal space. *But here's the key: when taken to an extreme, any trait can reverse its meaning.*

The handwriting of poet Emily Dickinson is an example of extreme letter and word spacing.

Too-wide spaces between letters with squashed letters as below is made by someone who has a strong need for solitude. It is nearly impossible for him to reach out to others, and he may appear withdrawn and self-protective. He underestimates the obstacles to achieving his aims, and may be wasteful.

Think of it this way—both very light pressure and very heavy pressure can be signs of anger. Yet, the expression of that anger is entirely different. One is passive or repressed, the other is explosive or aggressive. The same principle applies to spacing: it's not just the distance that matters, but the psychological intent and pattern behind it.

Narrow letter spacing is an expression of social tension and anxiety. The writer feels nervous, fearful and struggles to behave appropriately in social settings. This constriction of space mirrors an internal buildup of emotional pressure—one that, over time, may lead an explosive outburst. When letters are so tightly spaced that they consistently bump up against each other, and especially *when supported by other confirming signs*, it points to deep emotional distress, including suicidal ideation and/or a potential for violence or self-harm.

Extremely variable letter spacing signals ambivalence. The writer fluctuates between impulsivity and hesitation—rushing into things one moment, only to pull back the next. This inconsistency reveals self-doubt and inner conflict, making the writer's behavior difficult to predict.

Word Spacing

All areas of life ebb and flow—and social interaction is no exception. We move forward to engage with others, then pull back to recharge our emotional batteries. In speech, we pause for breath; in writing we pause through spacing. Just as some people speak rapidly, barely stopping to inhale, and others speak slowly and deliberately, leaving generous gaps between their words, these speech patterns are often mirrored in their handwriting. The way we space our words reflects not only how we communicate but how we relate to the world around us.

Word spacing is an unconscious area of handwriting—something we do automatically, without deliberate thought. The amount of space between words is a good indicator of the writer's physical and social distance. While other indicators, such as letter spacing and middle zone width, also contribute to this picture, word spacing provides a clear snapshot of the writer's personal boundaries.

As a general rule, the space between words should be approximately the width of a letter m *in that particular handwriting sample.*

Balanced word spacing represents healthy and balanced social needs—provided other factors in the handwriting support it. The writer is socially appropriate, knowing when engage with others and when to step back. Comfortable with both interaction and solitude, this individual respects boundaries—both their own and those of others.

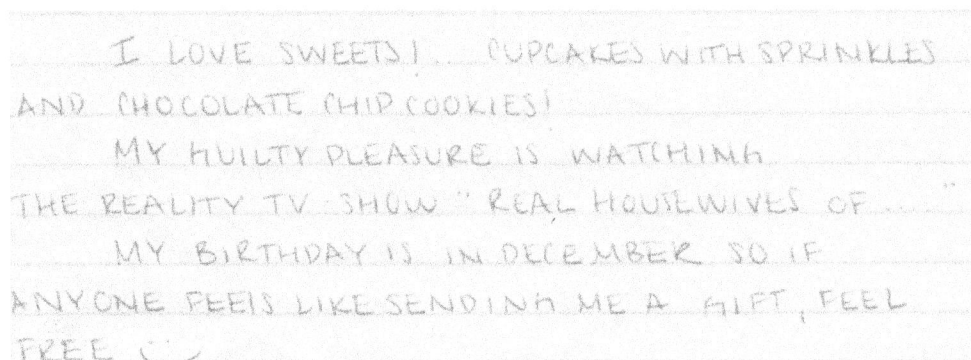

The narrower the word spacing, the more the impulsive the writer is. This type of person tends to intrude on others' personal space, both emotionally and physically. He may not recognize social cues that signal it's time to end a conversation or leave. In face-to-face interactions, he likely stands too close, perhaps even touching others without realizing it makes them uncomfortable—especially if the other person prefers more physical distance. This lack of spatial awareness can be unintentionally off-putting.

46

I ENJOYED HAVING THE OPPORTUNITY TO MEET YOU AS WELL AS HAVING YOU RIDE ALONG. I FOUND YOUR CONVERSATION AND KNOWLEDGE OF YOUR HANDWRITING ANALYSIS VERY INTERESTING. THANKS FOR COMING IN.

Extremely narrow word spacing occurs when words are written so closely that they touch, or nearly touch. The writer who lacks a sense of personal boundaries is uncomfortable with being alone. Surrounding himself with people indiscriminately, quantity of friendships is prioritized over quality.

Socially, this individual may dominate conversations with a voluble style leaves little room for others to get a word in edgewise. His need to express his views overrides sensitivity to whether others are actually interested.

When he is not the center of attention, his anxiety rises—he relies heavily on external approval to maintain his self-image and sense of worth.

I have been working for a label company for the past 6 months in a position that was represented to me as outside sales. It has turned into an inside sales position—which is why I'm writing you this letter.

---

*The larger the space **between** words, the more the writer pulls away from others and into himself.*

Wide word spacing—greater than the width of a letter *m* in that handwriting sample but not extreme—indicates a strong need for personal space, privacy, and time alone. The writer desires independence and, especially when wide line spacing is also present, is socially reserved.

47

This type of writer tends to observe the world through a more objective, intellectual lens rather than responding emotionally. Cautious and deliberate, he takes his time before reacting, preferring to process events internally. Interactions are thoughtful. Particularly in emotionally charged situations, he may come across as distant or detached. This makes sense for the sample below, which was written by a journalist who writes for a major magazine.

Extremely wide word spacing—greater than the width of two letter m's in that handwriting sample—signals difficulty with communication. Not only is it difficult for this writer to talk to others, but also to organize his thoughts clearly. Like the proverbial absent-minded professor, he may have a wealth of ideas but finds it challenging to articulate them coherently.

In social situations, the writer is likely to freeze up—especially if narrow letters and a wide right margin is also present—leading to awkward interactions or unintended blunders when he does speak. The larger the space between words, the greater the discomfort with social engagement, reflecting a tendency to retreat inward and avoid interpersonal connection. Interestingly, the sample below was written by a TV personality. The strong right slant of the writing (we will cover slant later) and some of the other elements of his writing make it possible to do his behind-the-scenes job.

48

As discussed earlier in the section on Spatial Arrangement, you may see a pattern of space going down the page known as 'rivers,' which signals an inner emotional split. The sample below demonstrates this pattern. although you can't clearly see the writing, the sample illustrates how rivers might look on a full page. The writer was serial killer Arthur Shawcross, but most people who form rivers are not criminals.

49

Lesson Four
Margins

Now that you've been introduced to the concept of figure/ground and its role in the overall spatial arrangement in handwriting, we turn to the individual elements that comprise it: margins, space between letters and words, line spacing, and baseline.

Margins symbolize

- how the writer uses his resources: time, money, energy

- the writer's experience of time: past and future

Like a picture frame, margins form the border of a handwriting sample. As the text progresses line by line down the page, the writer creates the left and right margins by moving the pen from one side of the paper to the other—left-to-right in English, or right-to-left in languages such as Hebrew or Arabic.

When they start out, a writer can't always predict how much space will remain at the end of a line. If there is more to say when space runs out, they must either hyphenate the final word or return to the left margin and choose where to begin the next line.

The start of each line is a more conscious choice than its end.

For this reason, we say the left margin represents the **ideal self**—the aspect of personality that makes deliberate choices based on the way he feels things *should* be. In contrast, the right margin represents the **real self**—the more spontaneous, unconscious self—the part that behaves instinctively and reveals how things *really* are.

51

In contemporary handwriting, top and bottom margins tend to receive less attention than left and right margins. Still, the top margin is generally expected to begin about two inches from the top edge of the paper. For the analyst, the key question is how consistent and balanced the margins are overall. The answer lies in the degree of control versus spontaneity expressed by the writer—and the margins offer one important clue.

Symbolism in Left and Right Margins

Handwriting carries a great deal of symbolism, particularly in the placement of margins. The left side of the page—where writing begins—symbolizes the past, origins, and new beginnings. The right side—where writing concludes—represents the future, endings, and the fulfillment of goals.

In this way, the movement across the page from left to right reflects a symbolic journey from past to future (interpretations can be flipped with Hebrew or Arabic writing). We can interpret the symbolism in a particular handwriting by examining two aspects of left and right margins:

1. The width of each margin and

2. The degree to which the lines of writing follow a similar pattern as they move down the page.

If the writer returns to more or less the same starting place at the end of each line, it creates a stable pattern down the left side of the page. Check how consistent the left margin is, or whether it becomes narrower or wider as it proceeds. Check the same for the right margin.

In business writing a one-inch wide margin all around is considered the norm. Therefore, depending on the paper size, a margin wider than one-inch is deemed "wide." A margin of less than one-inch is "narrow."

Despite the limited space available on a postcard, some writers still create margins—a subtle but telling indicator of their psychological makeup.

---

*The interpretations of the margin types that follow are intended as general guidelines and must be evaluated alongside other features present in the handwriting being analyzed. **It is less important to give an exact definition** to each margin type than to get a sense of their general meanings.*

52

Illustrations of various margins types appear at the end of this section

> *Reminder: Never interpret a single aspect of hand-writing. Always look at the gestalt—consider the context.*

Wide, balanced margins all around

Suggests good figure-ground balance in an orderly person who appreciates structure. Conserving space is not his first concern, which, depending on other elements might indicate generosity. In general, we infer that the writer is comfortable in the present, has made his peace with the past, and approaches the future with careful planning carefully.

Excessively wide margins all around

Usually found in conjunction with wide word and/or line spacing. Creates a **figure-ground imbalance**—too much 'ground' and not enough 'figure.' This may suggest a reluctance to engage in life. Imagine living on an island surrounded by a wide, water-filled moat—a symbolic barrier to keep others at a distance. Additional signs of isolation will typically be present.

With corroborating signs, may reflect unresolved issues from the past. Stuck in the moment, the writer avoids looking backward and resists moving forward (into the future).

Too-narrow margins all around

Creates the opposite type of **figure-ground imbalance.** In this instance there is too much 'figure' for the 'ground—the handwriting overtakes the space on the page. This individual doesn't know how to say no or when to quit. He tends to become over-involved with everything (and everyone) he takes on, and needs help properly setting priorities.

Too-narrow margins are interpreted similarly to overly wide ones, but the underlying behavior expresses itself differently. While both suggest a writer who is stuck in the present, the one with very narrow margins copes by filling time and space with people and activity—distractions to keep painful memories at bay.

53

Handwriting that presses against both the left and right edges of the page, leaving virtually no margins reveals an internal conflict: *the fear of moving forward held in tension with, and at the same time, a powerful urge to break free and make progress.*

Wide Margins

Moderately wide *left* margin

These are made by the shy writer who keeps a wide social distance, hesitating to extend himself emotionally or socially. Showing little interest in exploring his past, he is more inclined to move forward and create new experiences.

Extremely wide *left* margin

The writer may present an exaggerated image of generosity—one that is more appearance than substance. He appears uncomfortable with the past, pointing to unresolved or painful memories he would rather avoid. The tendency is to distance himself from those experiences, or even run from them entirely.

Moderately wide *right* margin

Typically made by the writer who demonstrates good taste and clear social boundaries. He is deliberate and forward-thinking, respectful of others' personal space and careful not to overstep uninvited.

Extremely wide *right* margin

When supported by other handwriting features, the writer may be shy and somewhat unrealistic in his view of the world. He finds it difficult to reach out to others, and likely perceived as reserved, perhaps even a bit paranoid. This margin displays anxiety about a future that he sees as uncertain or threatening.

Narrow Margins

Moderately narrow *left* margin

The writer is economical—cautious with time, money, and energy. The closer the writing hugs the left edge of the page, the more frugal the personality is likely to be.

This writer finds comfort in the past, perhaps cherishing long-standing friendships that may stretch back to childhood. Stepping outside his very narrow comfort zone is a challenge, and embracing new experiences does not come easily.

Moderately narrow *right* margin

The writer is spontaneous and enthusiastic—sometimes to the point of haste. Sociability and a desire to connect with others is also indicated. Future-focused, he moves forward with enthusiasm and optimism toward what lies ahead.

Extremely narrow *left* margin

The writer is likely to be a spendthrift with money, time, or other resources, only parting with any of them reluctantly. Change is intimidating, so he may be shy or fearful of venturing into the unknown, he sticks closely to what and whom he knows, preferring the safety of familiar people and routines.

No *right* margin

Where the writing pushes up against the edge of the page, it reflects the writer who doesn't always know when to quit. Propelled by a sense of urgency or eagerness about the future—perhaps excessively so—he is apt to run out of time, money, and other resources before completing what he starts. In certain cases, this type of margin has been observed in individuals with suicidal ideation, or in those facing terminal illness who have come to terms with their prognosis. *If this is true in the sample you are evaluating, it is crucial, to **exercise great caution** before making such an interpretation. Only consider it when supported by multiple corroborating features in the handwriting.*

No left margin

When writing begins at the very edge of the page it may, depending on supporting features, suggest a personality inclined toward hoarding. This writer clings tightly to his resources and the people in his life. He may be perceived as possessive or even greedy.

The absence of a left margin reveals deep-seated insecurity or anxiety tied to past experiences. By claiming ever bit of available space, the writer symbolically asserts control over his environment—a subconscious attempt to manage inner fear or uncertainty rooted in earlier loss or instability.

Margins with Other Shapes

Widening *left* margin

Where each line progressively pulls away from the left edge of the page, it suggests a writer who is fundamentally shy or reserved, yet compelled to step out into the world. There is a deliberate effort to engage socially or emotionally, or it may indicate someone swept up by enthusiasm or passion for their pursuits. In some cases, it points to emotional or financial extravagance. Psychologically, the widening left margin can signal a need to distance oneself from the past—moving forward with determination, perhaps even with a sense of urgency, in an effort to escape what lies behind.

Widening *right* margin

Each line pulls away from the right edge of the page. The writer becomes increasingly cautious the deeper he gets into new projects or activities. It's as if he's asking himself, "what have I gotten myself into?" and begins to retreat.

This behavior is rooted in emotional wounds or disappointments that inhibit forward momentum. The movement away from the right—symbolic of the future—reflects avoidance or anxiety about what lies ahead. The writer seeks comfort in the familiar, even if it no longer serves him, literally shrinking back from the future and seeking refuge in the past.

Shrinking *left* margin

When each new line starts closer to the left edge of the page, pulling back from the right edge—it indicates growing caution and a tendency to withhold. The writer may plunge into new experiences with enthusiasm, only to be overtaken by self-doubt or shyness that prompts a retreat.

This behavior reveals an internal conflict: the desire for engagement clashes with fear of exposure. The handwriting displays a gradual withdrawal—a symbolic pullback from the future. As the lines regress, the writer "pulls in his horns," signaling a growing reluctance to move forward, perhaps rooted in disillusionment, anxiety, or emotional fatigue.

Shrinking *right* margin

When each line moves progressively closer to the right edge of the page, the writer tries to restrain social or financial impulses, but is often swept up with growing enthusiasm. Despite initial efforts at control, the pull of excitement and anticipation about the future overrides caution. As time goes on, the writer's eagerness for what is to come intensifies. In combination with other signs, this type of margin indicates a general lack of self-regulation.

Concave *left* margin

The left margin pulls back and grows wider, then later retreats toward the left edge of the page. The concave shape reveals an internal struggle between boldness and fear. The writer begins with enthusiasm and forward momentum, eager to step into new territory. But as doubt creeps in, anxiety over having possibly made a wrong move triggers a sudden reversal, as retreating to safer ground. This margin pattern suggests a cycle of impulsivity followed by regret: advancing with confidence, then pulling back in caution—when it may be too late to turn around.

Concave *right* margin

The top and bottom lines of the text extend further to the right edge, causing the right margin to bow inward in the middle. The writer starts out with purpose, then hesitates mid-course. This moment of pulling back reflects uncertainty, overwhelm, or a lack of confidence. Yet, by the end, the writer regains momentum and moves forward again. This type of margin indicates someone who struggles with commitment or self-assurance at key points, but ultimately finds the resilience to press ahead.

Convex right margin

The lines at the middle of the page extend further right than those at the top and bottom, causing the margin to bulge outward. The writer's enthusiasm flares briefly before fading. The writing begins with restraint, then surges forward in a burst of excitement or inspiration, only to retreat once again into caution or self-restraint. This type of margin reflects emotional inconsistency: a cycle of initial hesitation, a short-lived surge of energy, and a return to inhibition. The writer may struggle to sustain momentum, often second-guessing themselves after the initial initial spark.

Convex left margin

Where the lines in the middle of the left side of the page extend further left than those at the top or bottom it suggests the writer who begins tentatively, quickly pulls back, then reconsiders and renews their efforts.

This pattern indicates early hesitation or fear, often stemming from self-doubt or uncertainty. The initial retreat reflects a desire to withdraw into a safe zone, but the eventual shift forward shows the writer's ability to summon the resolve to push on, despite his early misgivings. It represents a cycle of retreat and return—caution giving way to new resolve.

Variable *left* margin

Especially when the writing retreats past a clearly ruled left margin, it suggests a disregard for boundaries or conventional limits. The writer may be inclined to flout rules, resist authority, or operate outside accepted norms. In extreme cases, and when supported by other troubling indicators, this behavior may point to antisocial tendencies or even a predisposition toward criminal activity. At the very least, it reflects a strong-willed individual who resents constraints and insists on doing things their own way—regardless of expectation or structure.

Highly variable *right* margin

Some variability is natural and expected in the right margin, reflecting the normal fluctuations of mood and energy. However, when the variability becomes extreme, shifting erratically from wide to narrow, forward to back, it signals internal conflict.

The writer may struggle with moving forward in life, trying new things, or forming new relationships. This push-pull dynamic suggests a tension between desire and fear: the urge to engage clashing with an equally strong urge to retreat. The writer is conflicted about the future, caught up between excitement and anxiety about what lies ahead.

Highly regular *right* margin

This is an extreme and uncommon pattern, typically reflecting a profound need for control. The writer may feel compelled to dominate their environment, leaving little to chance or spontaneity.

When accompanied by supporting signs, it may point to underlying psychological disturbance or mental illness. Such rigid control can point to deep-seated fear, obsessive tendencies, or a fragmented sense of self that struggles to maintain internal order.

Upper and Lower Margins

Moderately spaced upper margin

The writer shows respect for the recipient, along with a sense of formality and reserve.

Too-wide upper margin

The writer may exhibit traits of extravagance and showiness, driven by a desire to appear more sophisticated or accomplished than they truly are. This need for outward display can mask underlying insecurities or a fear of being seen as ordinary. There is a concern with image and impression, a desire to be admired, more than truly known.

Narrow upper margin

The writer shows little concern for social niceties and tends to have an informal or indifferent attitude toward aesthetics. There may be a disregard for conventional standards of appearance or decorum. Unlike the writer who leaves a wide upper margin, this individual is more focused on practicality or personal comfort than on creating a visually pleasing environment. Their surroundings may appear cluttered, utilitarian, or simply lacking in cohesive taste.

Moderately spaced lower margin

The writer shows respect for the recipient. He is self-disciplined and good at planning ahead.

Narrow lower margin

The writer who ends the text at the very bottom of the page, leaving virtually no margin, demonstrates a lack of planning and foresight. This suggests spontaneity, impulsiveness, and a focus on immediate needs rather than long-term consequences.

There may also be a materialistic streak in someone grounded in the tangible, physical world. Rather than relying on external structures or guidance, the writer draws deeply on personal experience and inner reserves, often trusting instinct over logic.

Very wide lower margin

The writer may be hesitant or even fearful when it comes to exploring deep emotions—and this reluctance may extend to matters of sexuality. There's a tendency to intellectualize or idealize rather than fully engage with the physical or emotional self.

An idealist at heart, he prefers the world of thoughts, dreams, or spiritual aspirations over concrete realities. As a result, his "feet are not planted firmly on the ground," and he may struggle with practical concerns or establishing emotional intimacy.

Reminder: as with all other elements, these interpretations must be viewed within the context of the whole picture. Nothing stands alone. Yes, this is repetitious, and it bears repeating.

On the following pages are examples of some of the margins described in this section and a summary Margin Reference Guide.

1. Wide right margin

2. Narrow right margin

3. Widening left margins

4. Narrowing left margin

61

5. Narrowing right margin

6. Widening right margin - Narrowing left

7. Concave left, variable right

8. Straight left margin

9. Convex left margin

10. Convex right margin

11. Concave left margin, narrowing right

12. Concave right margin

63

13. Broad all around

14. Narrow all around

15. Variable left and right

16. Violates printed left margin

64

Margin Shape Reference Guide

Margin Type	Description
Moderately Wide Left	Shy, keeps wide social distance; hesitant to extend emotionally or socially. Shows little interest in exploring the past, ready to move forward.
Extremely Wide Left	May appear generous but is often avoiding painful past memories. Tends to distance or run from the past.
Moderately Narrow Left	Economical with time, money, and energy. Comfortable in the past, maintains long-term friendships, resists new experiences.
Extremely Narrow Left	Hoarding tendencies, insecure, clings to familiarity. May indicate shyness or fear of new experiences.
No Left Margin	Possessive, anxious about the past, seeks control by using all available space. Rooted in fear or early instability.
Widening Left Margin	Starts shy but makes effort to engage. Can show enthusiasm or emotional extravagance, distancing from the past with urgency.
Concave Left Margin	Begins confidently, then retreats. Suggests impulsivity followed by regret; fear emerges mid-effort.
Convex Left Margin	Tentative start, quick retreat, then renewed effort. Indicates caution followed by determination.
Moderately Wide Right	Good taste, clear boundaries, respectful of others. Deliberate and forward-thinking.
Extremely Wide Right	Shy, may have unrealistic worldview. Anxious about the future, appears reserved or even paranoid.
Virtually No Right Margin	Overeager for the future, poor planning, may run out of resources. In rare cases, linked to suicidal ideation or terminal illness (requires caution).
Right Margin Pullback	Lines pull away from right edge over time. Suggests withdrawal due to fear, uncertainty, or fatigue. Avoidance of future.
Lines Start Closer to Left	Initial enthusiasm fades into retreat. Conflict between desire for engagement and fear of exposure. Emotional fatigue or disillusionment.
Lines Get Closer to Right	Restrained start gives way to growing enthusiasm. May indicate poor self-control if combined with other signs.
Concave Right Margin	Begins with purpose, hesitates mid-way, then regains momentum. Suggests temporary self-doubt, followed by resilience.
Convex Right Margin	Restrained start, burst of enthusiasm mid-way, followed by retreat. Reflects emotional inconsistency and second-guessing.

Lesson Five
The Baseline

In handwriting analysis, the baseline refers to the invisible, or sometimes printed, line on which the writing rests. It is created by the bottoms of middle zone letters (such as a, e, s, etc.) and the connecting strokes—the ligatures—between them.

The baseline symbolizes the writer's progress toward his objectives and in some ways how successful he is at meeting them. The consistency with which letters return to the baseline contributes to the overall regularity of the writing—and reveals something important: the writer's need for security.

In contrast, the handwriting of someone who is more idealistic or emotionally detached may tend to float *above* the baseline—one thing that's more easily seen on lined paper. Writing above the baseline reflects a more visionary or abstract mindset—someone less grounded in practical concern and day-to-day realities of life.

The baseline can be evaluated in two main ways:

> *1. Consistency — how evenly the writing flows across the page,*

> *2. Direction — whether the baseline moves upward (ascending), downward (descending), remains relatively straight across the page, or wavers.*

Some variability in the baseline is not only acceptable, it's desirable. A **slightly variable** baseline suggests that the writer adapts to life's natural ebb and flow. Rather than clinging to a rigid structure, he allows for slight shifts in schedule and pace, leaving an opening to respond to changing circumstances, whether day to day or moment to moment.

> *Think of the baseline as symbolic ground—a stable foundation to stand on. A writer with a strong need for security needs to feel that solid footing beneath them.*

Assuming a well-formed lower zone and other positive features, the writer with a *slightly* variable baseline is generally able to stay on task and meet responsibilities on time. He is flexible and resilient, adapting well to last minute change. Last minute adjustments or occasional postponements don't throw him off course; he can shift gears without becoming overly distressed.

> *The greater the variability in the baseline, the easier it is to knock the writer off course.*

A very variable (wavy) baseline indicates a writer who is easily distracted and struggles with decision-making—or following through once a decision is made. When the baseline is extremely variable as shown below, it is a characteristic of moodiness, and in some instances emotional instability, especially when variability is echoed throughout the gestalt.

Writers with this type of baseline lack consistency. If you make plans with them, it's wise to confirm shortly beforehand—they may have changed their minds, forgotten, or simply drifted away from the original commitment. Reliability is not their strong suit.

68

Ruler writing: At the other end of the spectrum, you may occasionally encounter a baseline so straight it appears mechanical. The writer probably used a ruler, or even placed it on top of a printed line. While being goal-oriented is typically a positive trait, this kind of rigidity signals inflexibility. The writer's life is meticulously planned, with little room for spontaneity or contingency.

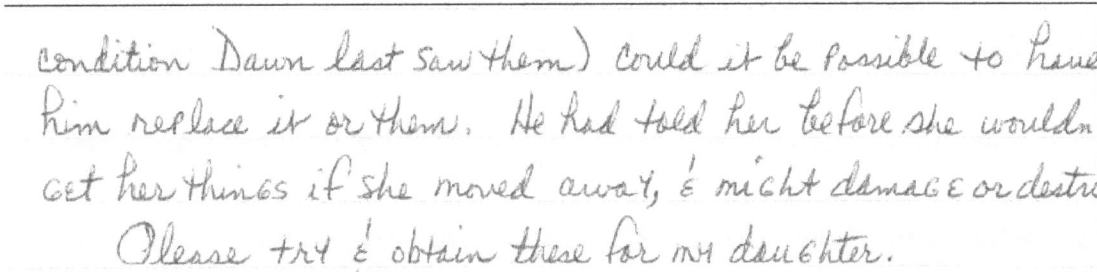

condition Dawn last saw them) could it be possible to have him replace it or them. He had told her before she wouldn't get her things if she moved away, & might damage or destru Please try & obtain these for my daughter.

A **rigid baseline** is a sign of tremendous underlying anxiety. The writer is afraid to let go, to act spontaneously, or to relinquish even a sliver of control. The structure he imposes on the baseline provides a fragile sense of security that allows him to believe he is in control of his environment—but that control hangs by a thread. Beneath the surface lies a fear of emotional unraveling if the baseline—this symbol of structure and order—is disrupted.

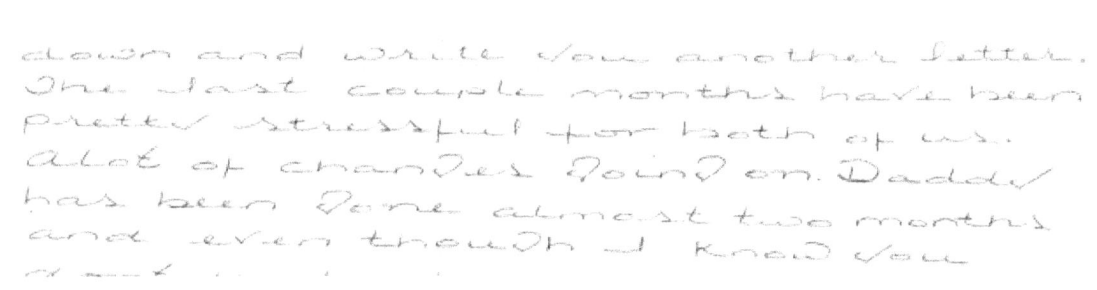

down and write you another letter. The last couple months have been pretty stressful for both of us. Alot of changes going on. Daddy has been gone almost two months and even though I know you

Think of a tightrope walker relying on a balancing pole to cross from one side to the other. Even then, the tightrope has some give in it. The writer of a rigid baseline, however, cannot tolerate even that much uncertainty.

The Baseline and Time

In addition to revealing goal-directedness, the baseline serves as a symbolic divider between past, present, and future. It functions as a line of demarcation, with the baseline itself representing the present moment. Above the invisible line lie the middle and upper zones, which symbolize the present and the future. Below it, in the lower zone, past experiences reside. (The concept of zones will be explored in a later lesson.)

We begin writing at the left margin, which represents the initiation of a goal, and move toward the right margin, the point of completion. This movement across the page mirrors the writer's journey toward achieving his goals. Along the way, the trail of ink tells its own story. We ask the writing: does the writer stay on course, or does the line rise, or fall as he veers off, or does it fluctuate, suggesting distraction, emotional turbulence, or difficulty staying focused?

In this way, handwriting becomes a form of symbolic time-travel. As the pen moves above and below the baseline, the writer shifts between past, present, and future, dipping into the lower zone to access past experiences and insights, then brings that knowledge up into the middle zone to apply it in practical ways in his daily life.

Think of the baseline as symbolic ground—a stable foundation to stand on. A writer with a strong need for security needs to feel that solid footing beneath them.

A handwriting that **hugs the baseline** like the sample below indicates a strong need to keep one's feet on the ground.

Baseline Alignment

The direction the baseline takes is much like body language—it offers subtle but important clues about the writer's emotional state. When you're feeling happy and confident, your posture reflects it: chin up, shoulders back, maybe even a smile. But after bad news, a rough day, or illness, your body tends to slump—shoulders droop, eyes downcast, energy fades. Your whole body seems to sag.

In handwriting, the baseline behaves the same way. It reflects the writer's attitude towards life at the moment of writing. Since emotions and circumstances naturally shift to some degree from day to day, it may not be possible, but would be ideal to review the baselines in handwriting samples written over a period of time. This broader perspective can provide a more accurate picture of the writer's general outlook.

It makes sense that someone who is energetic, optimistic, and projects warmth and enthusiasm would write with a slightly ascending (uphill) baseline. This person's internal buoyancy—his ability to rebound quickly from setbacks—keeps him moving forward with a positive outlook. The baseline below moves strongly uphill, but the overall gestalt is okay.

Think of the myth of Sisyphus, the Greek king condemned to push a massive boulder up a hill for eternity, only to watch it roll back down each time he neared the top. That's the emotional landscape of the writer with a *steeply* ascending baseline: a forced optimism masking deep inner effort and exhaustion.

71

He keeps telling himself, 'if I just keep pushing, tomorrow things will get better.'

Note: an extreme uphill slant is not a sign of true optimism. Instead, the writer feels they are fighting an uphill battle, struggling to maintain a positive mental outlook.

By contrast, a descending baseline is usually seen in someone who feels tired, discouraged, unwell, depressed, or has a consistently pessimistic outlook. The download slope of the baseline reveals a loss of momentum, as if he's being pulled down by the weight of his own despondency. This writer lacks the emotional—and perhaps the physical energy or belief—that things will get better and he'll be able to pick himself up.

As always in such a case, it's important to look at multiple handwriting samples written over a period of time before reaching a conclusion. A temporary slump in mood may show up in the writing, but only a *pattern* of descending baselines over time can help to determine whether this gloomy attitude is situational, or part of a deeper, more enduring personality trait.

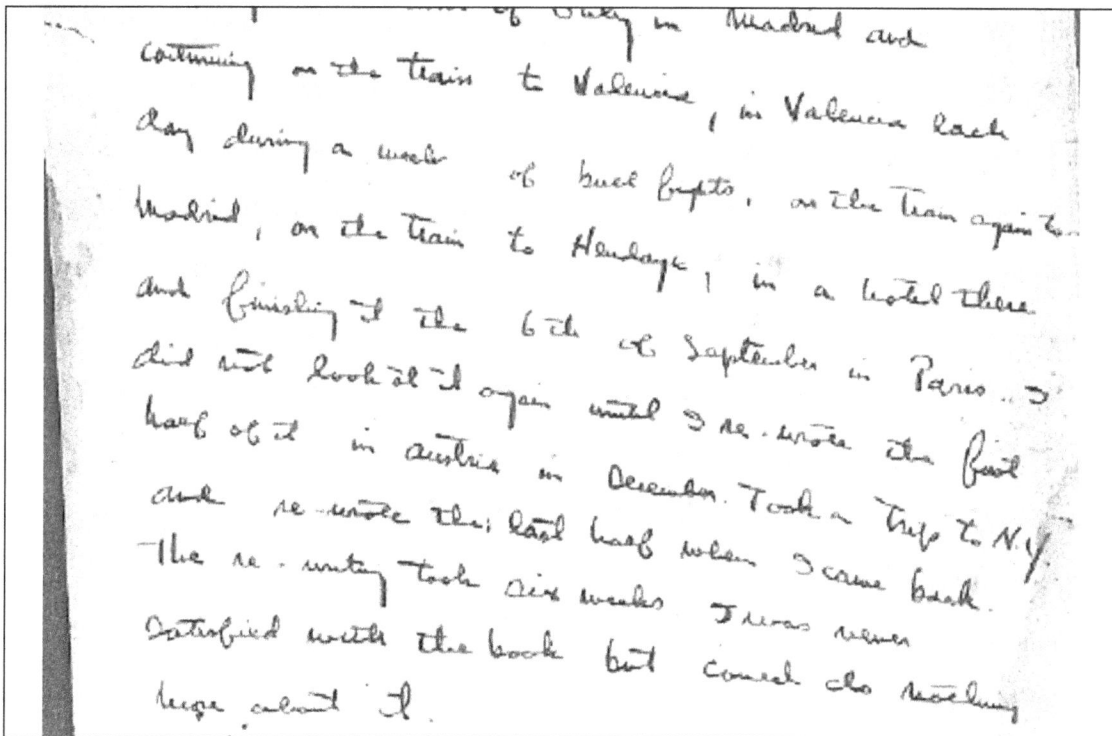

Ernest Hemingway

An extreme downhill slant can appear in the handwriting of individuals experiencing severe depression—and in some cases, are thinking about suicide. A well-known example is Ernest Hemingway, where the baselines in his final writings dipped deeply as he neared the end of his life.

Paradoxically, though, the reverse may also be true. Once a suicidal person has made the decision to follow through, a sense of relief or even elation—the belief that the end of their hopelessness is in sight—can result in a sharply *ascending* baseline. This is another important reminder of why no single ele-

73

ment of handwriting should ever be interpreted in isolation. It is essential to consider the full context and look for supporting signs in the writing.

A **convex baseline** rises in the middle and curves downward toward the end, forming a gentle hill shape. It often accompanies a convex right margin and suggests a writer who starts off with initial enthusiasm and high hopes, but whose energy dwindles as he becomes more deeply involved in a project or a relationship. What begins with eagerness may taper off as motivation fades.

In contrast, the **concave baseline** sags in the middle and then rises again—like a shallow valley. This type of baseline indicates someone who makes a slow start, beginning with hesitation or low energy, but who gathers momentum as they go. Once fully engaged, this writer tends to build enthusiasm over time and is likely to follow through to completion.

Another type of baseline is the **step-up or step-down** pattern, where individual words, rather than the entire line, form their own rising or falling baseline. In the following handwriting you can see an example of both, as well as an overall strongly rising (ascending) baseline.

In the **step-up** pattern, a word begins at the baseline and rises above it, making the whole word slant. This is distinct from a baseline where the entire sentence or line ascends. The writer of the step-up pattern feels spurts of tremendous enthusiasm or hopefulness but tries to keep it in check, as if by restraining or moderating his excitement it will stop him from becoming emotionally exposed.

The **step-down** pattern is the opposite—single words descend. The writer is constantly struggling to pull himself up and stay positive, but feels weighed down, as if each step forward is a challenge. Despite great effort, maintaining motivation may feel like an uphill battle that he can never quite win.

It is sometimes instructional to look at the words that are descending, as they may offer clues to what is in the writer's mind, causing him to struggle.

Finally, a baseline may appear reasonably straight as it crosses the page, but then—as it reaches the right margin—the final word, or even part of a word, **crashes into the edge of the paper** and falls down. This is the mark of a poor planner who may start out strong but fails to anticipate what's needed to reach the finish line. This writer is likely to run out of resources—

75

time, energy, or money—because he hasn't looked far enough ahead. His sense of realism is clouded by extravagance over overconfidence. Consequently, he is likely to find himself scrambling to complete what he began with such enthusiasm.

Measuring the Baseline

Place a ruler on a copy of a page of writing—don't mark up the original!—Place the left edge of the ruler at the bottom of the first letter on the line and the right edge under the last letter of that line of writing. Draw a line between the two points. This technique tells you the direction of the baseline: straight across, rising, or falling.

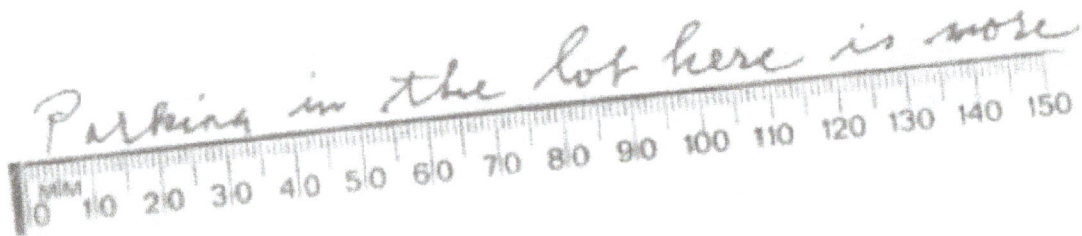

Measuring line direction using the rising handwriting of comedian Shelly Berman.

Measuring Across the Baseline

Again, using a copy, place the ruler on the bottom of the first letter and lay it straight across the page so that the ends of the ruler touch the left and right edge of the paper. Draw a line to see whether the letters and words return to the baseline, rise above it, or fall below it. In the following illustration, the writing is regular, sticking close to the baseline.

Measuring across the baseline.

76

PART TWO
Form

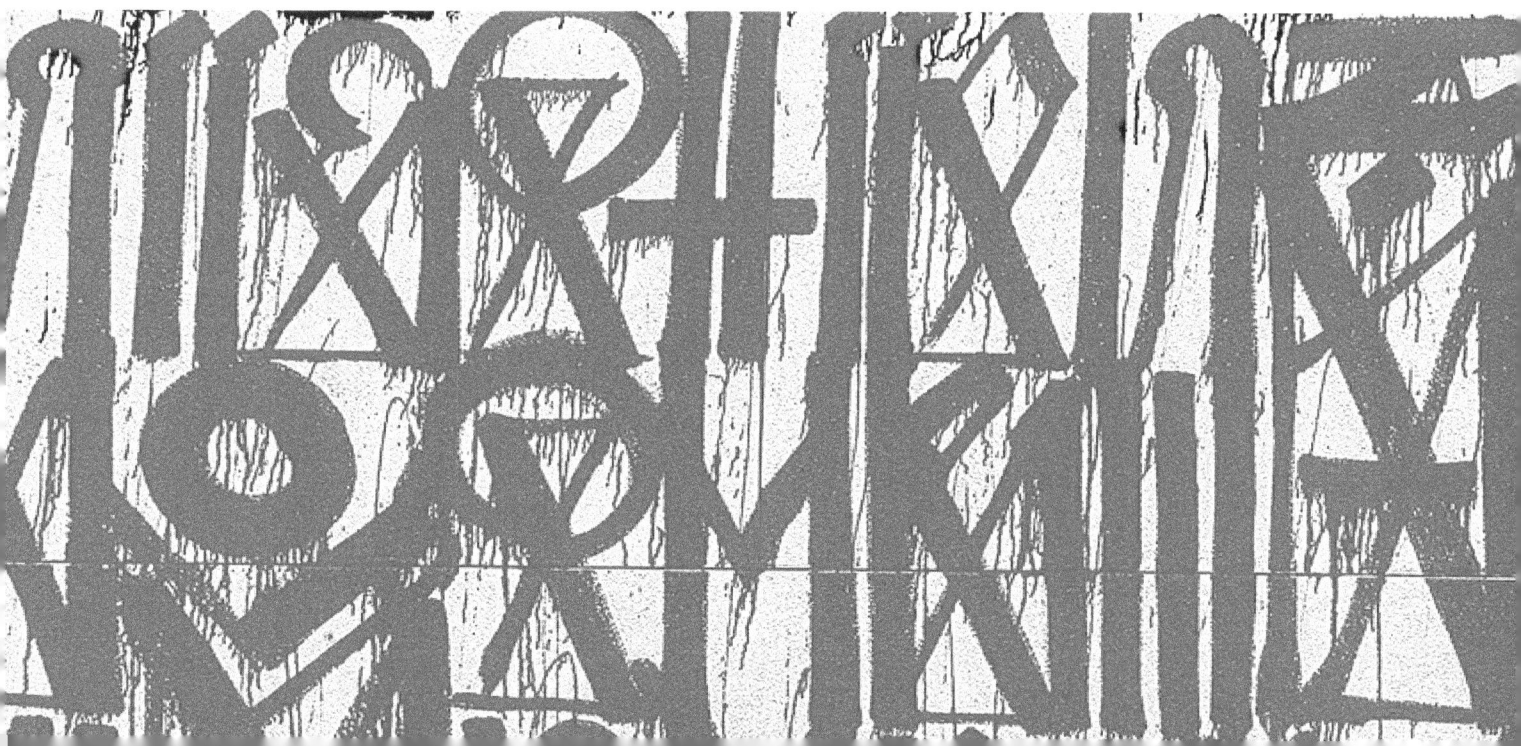

Lesson Six
Introduction to Form

A person's handwriting is shaped by a combination of psychological and developmental influences that include temperament, environment, and life experiences. However, those personal variations come later. Around third grade, most children are taught a specific copybook handwriting style, which provides a standardized foundation.

Every country has its own national copybook, and many—like the United States—have more than one. Because handwriting is typically analyzed in comparison to the model the writer originally learned, it is essential for professional analysts to be familiar with a variety of national styles. With practice, you may be able to recognize where a writer was educated—such as in England Eastern Europe, France, or the Philippines, for example—based solely on the features of their handwriting. Google Images can be a helpful resource for locating copybooks from many countries, as is the American Handwriting Analysis Foundation library (available for its members).

In the U.S., older adults often learned Palmer or Zaner-Bloser. During the 1970s, D'Nealian—a more fluid, simplified script—was introduced. In recent years, methods such as CursiveLogic© and New American Cursive© have emerged. Although there are other options on the market, these two are the most developmentally appropriate from a graphological perspective.

Personality determines the writing style that the child, and later the adult, chooses for written communication

79

Learning to write requires the child to develop an entirely new skill set, involving intense concentration and motor coordination. The process begins with forming individual letters, then combining them into words, and eventually, constructing full sentences and paragraphs.

Once the child can write fluently without conscious effort, we say they have reached a degree of *graphic maturity*—meaning they now have the freedom to modify and personalize their handwriting Some individuals retain the school copybook model into adulthood because it feels familiar and comfortable. Others embellish their writing, either for aesthetic reasons or to express individuality. Some simplify it, omitting unnecessary loops or flourishes. Still others choose to print, particularly among students educated under the 2009 Common Core Curriculum, which short-shortsightedly removed the requirement to teach cursive.

The good news is that more than half of U.S. states have responded to the unintended consequences of this decision by reinstating handwriting instruction. Several more have legislation pending.

How Space, Form, and Movement Work Together

In Part One, space was conceptualized as the structural framework within which handwriting *forms* are organized. An in-depth discussion of *movement*—element that strongly impacts form—will follow in Part Three. At this stage, it's enough to recognize that space, form, and movement are inextricably linked and interrelated. **Space** provides the environment in which movement occurs. **Movement** gives shape to form. **Form**, in turn, reflects the interaction between both. A thorough understanding of these interrelationships provides a more coherent and integrated picture of personality, making handwriting analysis clearer and more meaningful.

We have already discussed the concept of figure/ground distribution, where the paper on which you write was described as symbolic of the ground, and the spatial arrangement of the ink is the symbolic *figure* on that background. *Form*, which we cover next, is the way the figure looks—its design or style.

80

Generally speaking, one whose handwriting is *ground-dominated* (it has more white space) is more intellectually-driven (note: this does not necessarily mean more intelligent or smarter).

In a more emotionally-driven writer, the *figure is dominant* (the writing takes over the white space). As always, look for balance between the two. If the gestalt is unbalanced, we seek the reasons why.

Extremes at either end of the emotion-intellect
spectrum generally produce a negative or 'disturbed' gestalt.

Dictionary Definitions of Form

- *The shape and structure of an object*

- *Manners or conduct as governed by etiquette, decorum, or custom*

- *Method of arrangement or manner of coordinating elements*

Let's examine those definitions one at a time:

— *Shape and structure of an object: form is the style the writer chooses for self-expression. It might be school copybook, or it might be simplified, elaborated, printed, etc. Form is also the shape of the letters, which gives the handwriting structure.*

— *Manners or conduct as governed by etiquette, decorum, or custom: form reveals something about the writer's ego as revealed by his social conduct and how much (or how little) emphasis is placed on tradition, manners, courteous behavior, or pretension, etc.*

— *Method of arrangement or manner of coordinating elements: as the figure against a background, the form reveals how the intellect and emotions interact in the writer's environment.*

The function of handwriting is communication, which
means choosing a style (form) that works to that end

81

Understanding Form: Style, Intention, and Function

Basically, form or style is the way the writing looks. It could be compared to font choice on a computer. While the *spatial arrangement* is an unconscious choice, the *form* the handwriting takes is a more conscious one. Some writers will select a particular writing style because they like the way it looks. Others don't care, and their writing style shows it.

In the world of design, a core principle is that 'form follows function'—meaning the shape and structure of an object (handwriting) should serve a practical purpose—the design should reflect what the object is meant to do (communicate), not simply reflect aesthetics.

In handwriting analysis, whatever style the writer chooses must support its primary function–communication. If the writing is illegible or overly ornamented, it fails to serve that function, no matter how stylish or distinctive it may appear.

Form in handwriting represents ego development and the writer's presentation of self to the world. Ask yourself: Does the 'stylishness' of the handwriting form draw the eye to such a degree that the viewer is distracted from the purpose of the communication?

Shapes in Handwriting

All handwritten forms are comprised of a series of curved lines and straight lines. Traditionally, curves represent *femininity* and the qualities of yieldingness, softness, nurturing and loving, emotionality, responsiveness. Straight lines represent *masculinity*, which includes such qualities as toughness, assertiveness, intellectual orientation.

In the twenty-first century, gender lines are more blurred than they once were. Rather than gender, handwriting reveals those traditional qualities of masculinity/femininity. Some men are more tender-hearted and their handwriting reflects it. Some women are tougher-minded and it shows in their

82

handwriting, too. Everything in handwriting is seen along a continuum, so it's all a matter of degree.

An over-emphasis on curved lines is found in a more emotionally-based writer whose ego is not well developed. An over-emphasis on straight lines is made by one who prefers to strip away emotion and view things intellectually.

Curves and Emotion

The next sample demonstrates rounded forms. The crowded lines weaken the spatial arrangement, leaving the gestalt (overall picture) disturbed.

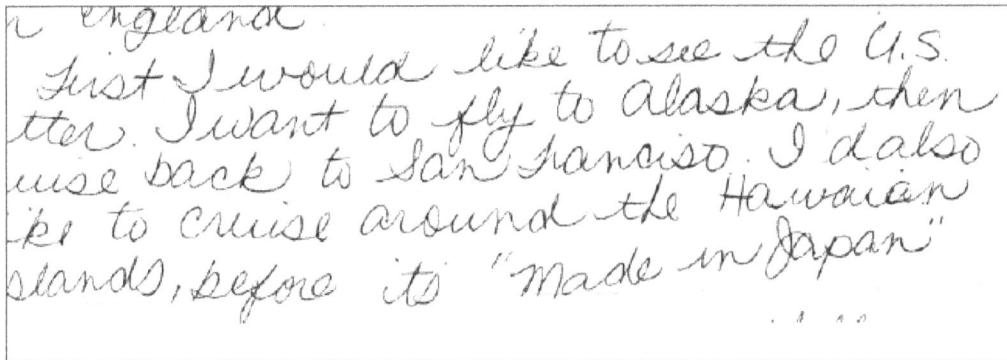

The writer views the world through an emotional lens. The weak (overall crowded) spatial arrangement reveals a subjective perspective–she interprets situations based on how they affect her personally, with a happy-go-lucky refusal to look at the negative in any situation. For this type of writer, stepping back to see the bigger picture is a challenge. With a little more objectivity, she could make more balanced judgments and decisions.

Straight Lines and Intellect

A predominance of straight lines creates a linear appearance, indicating a more intellectually-oriented writer. The sample below displays a balanced spatial arrangement that contributes to a good gestalt. Notably, the *letters* are narrow in an overall balanced spatial arrangement, and the simplified letter forms are well-developed. While the writing is on the linear end of the spectrum, the presence of some rounded forms provides a counterbalance, maintaining overall harmony—a good gestalt.

With a good spatial arrangement, the linear writer plans ahead and efficiently manages his time. Perceptive, observant, and objective, he carefully considers cause and effect, and anticipates the consequences of his actions.

He has little patience for what he sees as superficial social interactions unless they serve a clear purpose. The block printing sample of astronaut Alan Bean, next, is overly angular, which results in a disturbance of *form*. As an astronaut, maintaining a cool-headed, intellectual demeanor is essential. This handwriting reflects a suppression of emotional responses.

The dominance of straight strokes in left slant with a lack of balancing curves indicates that he keeps his emotional life under wraps. This pattern is quite common among individuals in military and paramilitary roles, such as law enforcement, where calm, rational behavior is critical, but often comes at the expense of emotional balance.

The clear spatial arrangement contributes positively to the gestalt, revealing clear thinking and planning ability, but the dominance of straight lines and sharp angles creates a form imbalance and results in a disturbance in the gestalt. In addition, the left slant reveals a need to move away from others, making the writer uncomfortable in social settings.

Although our current discussion centers generally around form—particularly curves and straight lines—a more detailed examination of connective forms (garland, arcade, angle, thread and their subtypes) will be covered in Lesson 10. In the meantime, it's clear that this handwriting features numerous linear strokes forming acute angles, with very few rounded corners. This indicates stubbornness and resistance to outside influence.

Lesson Seven
Strong-Weak-Disturbed Continuum

Just as we did with the spatial arrangement in Part One, the gestalt graphologist's task is to evaluate where the writing form falls on the strong, weak, or disturbed continuum. Next, we asses whether form has been emphasized at the expense of function—that is, whether the visual style of the writing is so attention-grabbing that it draws the eye away from the message and detracts from its primary purpose: communication.

Each of the points along the continuum spotlights different personality characteristics and levels of functioning, depending on the context of the particular handwriting in which it is found. **Weak** form adheres to copybook style. In s**trong** form, copybook has been improved by *simplifying* the writing in positive ways. In **disturbed** form, letter designs have broken down, are poorly made, or at the other extreme are overly embellished. These will all be discussed at length in the following section.

To qualify as **strong** *form, a handwriting must show originality by improving on the copybook model learned in school and retaining legibility.*

Positive *originality* may be achieved through various means. S*implification of form* being the easiest and most common:

- ◦ *Elaborate capital letters can be simplified*
- ◦ *Lead-in strokes at the beginnings of words can be omitted without loss of legibility*
- ◦ *Some loops can be replaced with simple downstrokes*

87

These small modifications are effective strategies that not only enhance legibility, but also increase writing speed. Writers who eliminate these superfluous strokes communicate more efficiently as their handwriting becomes clearer and quicker to produce.

A simplified handwriting is much like this minimalist piece of art: reduced to its essentials, yet still fully expressive. The viewer immediately grasps the intended message or feeling because nothing extraneous distracts from the core meaning the artist wants to convey.

Like the artwork, a simplified handwriting achieves a good **gestalt** because all the elements are balanced, cohesive, and harmonious. Everything fits together naturally, and nothing needs to be added or altered to "make it right."

A reasonable degree of simplification contributes to **strong form** and shows initiative, intelligence, and sound decision-making. When it appears in a strong spatial arrangement, simplification of form generally reflects a goal-directed, critical thinker who is quick to understand the facts without a lot of superfluous details.

Simplification in handwriting reduces *form-consciousness*, which we will cover in this lesson, rather than reinforcing it. When the writer makes deliberate, positive choices to eliminate unnecessary elements, such as extra initial and final strokes, ornate capitals, superfluous loops, or excessive connections, the result is increased speed and efficiency.

Too much simplification destroys the form and makes the writing less legible.

Extreme Simplification

As in every other aspect of writing, any extreme interferes with legibility. When handwriting is simplified to an extreme degree, legibility suffers, and this may signal underlying personality disintegration. This is usually is not

88

due to conscious choice, but may be a result of extreme stress and sometimes mental illness. However, there can be exceptions.

The next handwriting sample demonstrates a good overall gestalt due to its balanced spatial arrangement. Yet, a closer examination reveals that the writing is largely illegible because the extreme simplification has broken down the form. How would you interpret this? In this case, the writer—a man in his sixties on the autism spectrum— presents a valuable reminder that context matters. Neurodivergent or medically complex individuals may produce handwriting that defies typical interpretation.

Jane Goodall

Key principle: When you encounter something highly unusual—such as handwriting that appears strong in form yet is illegible—a physical, mental, or emotional condition may be influencing the handwriting. You must seek additional information about the writer before proceeding with analysis. Without that critical context, your conclusions and interpretation may be accurate or misleading.

Neglect of form

Neglect of form signals a breakdown of the ego. This can be seen in the handwriting sample below, written by a woman frequently hospitalized for episodes of paranoid schizophrenia. She wrote letters to strangers, filled with

89

disorganized thoughts. The form is so neglected as to be skeletal—disintegrated—reflecting a psyche overwhelmed by psychological distress—a mind pushed beyond its ability to cope.

Contrast this with the previous sample from a man on the autism spectrum. The distinction between pathology and neurodivergence can sometimes only be made by reading the context and gathering additional information about the writer. Without it, we risk misinterpreting the sample.

Not all neglect of form stems from mental illness. A less extreme example, like the one below, may simply reflect exhaustion in someone feeling literally 'strung out' due to an intense work schedule. Or a single parent trying to care for a family while also working more than one job. The handwriting belongs to an author on a grueling book tour, signing more than a hundred books at a time. There was no time or energy for aesthetics.

Strong Form

Simplified and balanced in its distribution of curved and straight lines, strong form has a natural—*though not perfect*—appearance. The form itself does not stand out in a way that draws the eye to its pictorial quality, and nei-

90

ther is it disturbed, in which case the letters would be poorly formed and unattractive, as we will see further in this lesson.

A writer who demonstrates *strong* form typically learned to adapt successfully to their environment. The departure from copybook through simplification, originality, or personal stylization, indicates confidence and a willingness to express individuality and create his own lifestyle.

Handwriting with strong form will always show at least some degree of simplification.

Such writing points to good imagination and a well-developed inner life. When plans don't go as expected, this writer possesses the emotional resilience to adapt and keep on going. Positive ego drive and ego strength supply the self-confidence necessary to meet his emotional needs.

Following is an example of strong form with strong space, too. What makes it strong? Overall good balance in the spatial arrangement, though the lines are a tad closer than they could be. The letter forms, simplified and attractive, don't draw attention to themselves, and they are mostly legible.

The writer is comfortable expressing feelings when appropriate, and knows how to restrain them when it is not. They have enough self-confidence that they are not compelled to draw attention to themselves in a way that turns heads and observers say, "what the heck was s/he thinking?"

91

Strong form does not necessarily mean a 'good' or 'nice' person, although it may.

The next sample was penned by famed psychiatrist Carl Jung. Strong form is evident in the simplification and there is strong movement, too. The word spacing, however, is narrow, and in some cases the pen is moving so quickly, the words connect. This reveals a quick, facile mind, but it disrupts the gestalt to some degree and indicates a potential weakness in interpersonal boundaries.

Carl Jung

Weak Form

We started the discussion of copybook writing in the last lesson. Now let's revisit it through the lens of form, where it is considered *weak*.

Simply put, in **weak** form no real effort has been made to individualize the letter forms; the handwriting remains largely unchanged from the style learned in school. Writers who retain copybook form prefer conformity over individuality. They seek to blend in with their chosen group rather than stand out. They feel more secure operating within established norms, gravitating toward familiar surroundings and routine tasks.

Next is a stereotypical copybook handwriting.

The writing may be pleasant enough, but it follows the old rules and conventions—just like its writer prefers to do. Writers who maintain copybook writing long into adulthood tend to cling to the past, sticking to what they know, doing things they way they have always been done. This suggests someone who is conservative in their views and may be less open to new information. Their most comfortable relationships are formed with those who think like them.

The sample below adheres closely to copybook style.

Marilyn Vos Savant

These individuals typically look for clear standards and regulations to follow, and may thrive in structured environments. Careers in teaching, nursing, and administration—fields that value consistency, reliability, and adherence to protocol—are especially well-suited to this personality type—and goodness knows, they are needed.

Understanding Weak Form

What makes *weak form* weak is its conventionality—the need to cling to the familiar, such as the school-taught model of writing, rather than evolving into a more original or expressive style. This reliance on tradition may reflect a lack of confidence and need for the security provided by well-established rules. It

93

may indicate an ego that is still in the process of development, or in some cases, one that has not fully matured.

The closer handwriting sticks to copybook form, the more likely the writer is to have a conventional and inflexible worldview—not only regarding their personal life but also how the external world "should" work. These writers generally content with the status quo, and prefer to keep things the way they have always been. Seeking approval from their chosen social group, they may adjust their behavior to conform to group norm—whether that social group are conventional friends, a gang, or some other.

It's important to note: copybook style is not inherently negative. Rather, it represents a particular personality orientation—one that values structure, tradition, and external validation over individuality or innovation.

Even when a handwriting sample appears to have a generally good gestalt, if the form is weak (copybook writing) and the spatial arrangement is also weak (spatially crowded), leaving little room for personal expression or dynamic flow, it will negatively impact the analysis.

Such writing merely *sits on the page*—static and lifeless. As seen in the following two samples, the disturbed gestalt results from the combination of conventional, undeveloped (weak) and an overall lack of dynamic movement in the writing. It may appear neat, but it lacks the individuality, energy, and balance that indicates psychological vitality. However, because the picture of space is good, the writer functions reasonably well in the world.

94

Here is another example of weak form in a weak (crowded) picture of space.

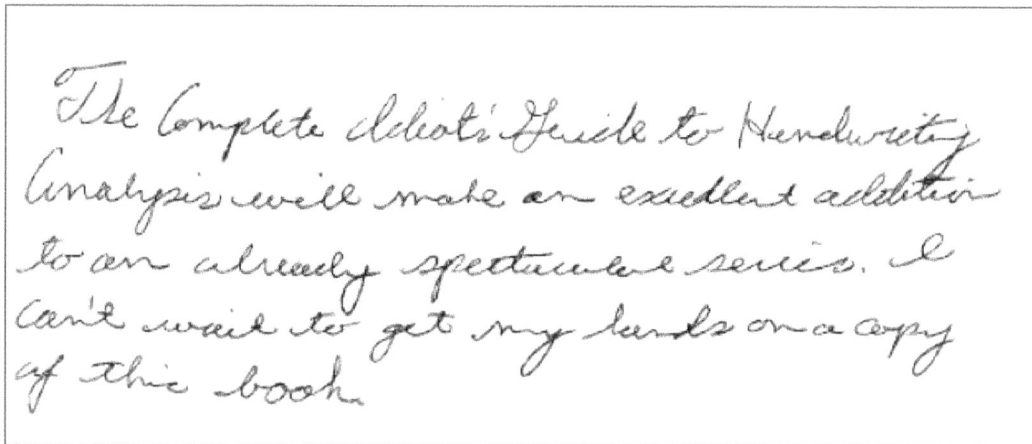

Many people admire the penmanship of older generations and say things like, "My mother has beautiful handwriting, just like she learned in school." What often comes as a surprise is that beautiful handwriting does not necessarily reflect a beautiful or well-adjusted personality (though it certainly can).

In fact, copybook style is frequently found in the handwriting of prison inmates and gang members. In such cases, the continued use of rigid, school-taught forms may indicate a deep need for structure—whether imposed by prison regulations, or the strict codes of gang affiliation—but not necessarily to society's broader moral or social norms.

Those who attended religious schools are more apt to maintain the copybook style of writing over their lifetime than public school students. This is at least in part because they were taught at a young age to conform to strict rules. Not all children who attend religious schools grow up sticking with copybook style, but a high percentage seem to. And, as mentioned above, many of these people work in service careers, such as administration, nursing, and school teaching, which attracts certain personality types—individuals who work well within an environment where structure and order are needed.

The next writing sample was made by an incarcerated gang member. There are some departures from copybook, but not positive ones. Though there are some strange letter forms, there is overall a lack of *positive* originality.

Hello, It's Me David writing you these few lines Down your way Hoping that when this Letter Reaches your Destination Jenifer, It May find you in the best of Everything and in Gods Most tender Loving care.

This sample has some positive departures from copybook.

This is a sample of my handwriting for our forum. Like those who prepare samples for me, I don't quite know what to say. Am I nervous about what you might say? A little.

Such individuals often depend on external sources for approval and direction. Rather than relying on internal judgment or self-guidance, they are more likely to look outward for leadership, reassurance, and a sense of belonging.

Note: the descriptions of copybook writers are general. It should go without saying that within copybook style, as with any other style, a wide range of behaviors may be found.

Disturbed Form

While all aspects of a handwriting sample offer insight into the writer's ego, **form** provides the most fundamental reflection of self-image—what the writer perceives when looking into their *psychic mirror*.

A solid foundation in personality theory is essential for fully understanding the implications of disturbed form. Ideally, this foundation should be supplemented with the formal study of psychology. For our purposes, what follows is a brief and simplistic discussion of the **ego and its functions** as it relates to form. The discussion of the ego, as well as the id and superego will continue in Lesson 8

Disturbed form occupies a class of its own. It cannot be categorized as either strong or weak, yet not strictly copybook either. Instead, it is often marked by exaggerated embellishments, oversized loops, decorative swirls, and unnecessary ornamentation that distorts the basic structure of the writing.

The primary motivation behind this style is the writer's **need to be seen**, to stand out from the crowd and demand recognition. Unfortunately, more often than not, the attention-grabbing behaviors associated with this drive for attention are often self-defeating. Rather than receiving positive validation, the writer is likely to attract negative attention due to disruptive or inappropriate actions.

The embellishments themselves disrupt the gestalt because the eye is drawn to the pictorial or decorative elements, which lack harmony or aesthetic appeal. These additions detract from clarity and balance, and ultimately undermine strong form.

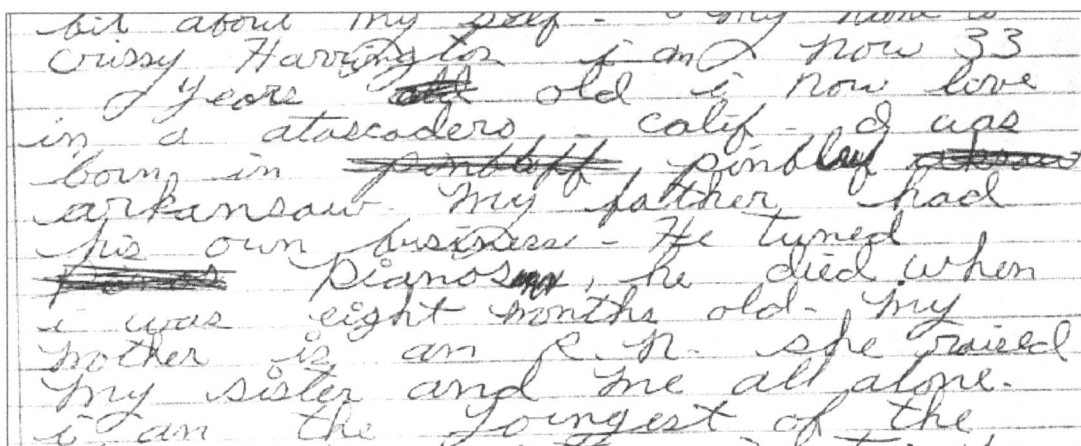

In a handwriting with **disturbed form**, something feels "off," even if you can't immediately identify what it is. A writer with disturbed form may get things done by sheer willpower, but their handwriting reveals underlying emotional struggles. This reflects internal imbalance and a poor self-image.

In the sample on the previous page, the disturbance in form is immediately evident. The eye is drawn to the undeveloped letter shapes and overall messiness, which is due to too much variability all over. When word spacing is wide and yet inconsistent, it points to challenges in social interaction—the writer wants to interact with others but holds back out of a fear that started early in childhood.

Additional problems with the writing *movement* (to be explored in Part 3) reinforce the impression of internal conflict and hesitancy.

Following is a sample of female serial killer, Christine Falling. Her handwriting serves as a powerful example of mixed weak and disturbed form.

Christine Falling

98

Form Consciousness

As we have said, strong form arises from positive departures from copybook. The writing appears natural and spontaneous, supporting the function of writing—communication. **Form consciousness**, however, is something else entirely. While strong form enhances expression, form consciousness emphasizes appearance over purpose. It draws attention to the handwriting itself rather than the message it conveys. This reverses the principle mentioned earlier, that *form should follow function.*

Does Really it Matter in Handwriting?

Yes. Because when the form becomes so elaborate or stylized that it draws attention away from the message, we must ask ourselves:

1. *Why is the writer trying to distract us?*
2. *What is the writer trying to hide?*

Handwriting that prioritizes aesthetic impact over clarity reflects a subconscious desire to conceal, impress, or manipulate how the writer is perceived. Beneath this **form consciousness** lie deep-seated personality conflicts. The writer fears their true self is unacceptable, so they construct a façade—using handwriting to present an idealized version of themselves.

The effort to produce polished or beautiful writing serves as a distraction, a way to keep others from looking too closely and seeing the real person beneath the surface. This type of handwriting is known as **persona writing**, a concept we will explore further in Lesson 8.

Sustaining such a mask requires continuous psychological effort. When the gap between one's outward presentation and inner reality grows too wide, it can lead to emotional strain—and, eventually, serious psychological disturbances.

Lesson Eight
Form and Ego

This lesson goes into further depth on how **form** in handwriting relates to the ego. We begin by exploring how the *id, ego,* and *superego* are represented not only in the three zones of handwriting but also how they affect the entire writing.

As always, remember that no single feature stands alone— every element must be considered within the context of the entire sample.

The Ego

The *ego* represents the conscious, reality-oriented part of the personality. It serves as the mediator between one's internal desires and the demands of the external world, regulating thought and behavior accordingly.

Often referred to as the "director" or adult aspect of the self, the ego operates on the *reality principle*, striving to balance impulses, morality, and practical needs. A mature individual is expected to use common sense, rational thinking, and the ability to see things as they truly are—not merely as they wish them to be. The ego is responsible for planning and regulating behavior through self-discipline, rather than through fear or threat.

A well-developed ego not only facilitates getting things done, but also considers the long-term consequences of contemplated actions. It is the ego that enables delayed gratification, striking a balance between two internal forces— the *id,* or "inner child," which demands, "I want what I want and I want it now!"—and the restrictions of the *superego,* or conscience, which says, "No, you can't have it."

101

Operating as the central regulator of the personality, the ego manages the energy that flows between the unconscious urges of the id and the moral constraints of the *superego*. Because the ego mediates between these forces, its influence can be seen throughout the handwriting—not just in isolated features.

A **strong ego** is seen in a good gestalt: the overall handwriting appears reasonably well-balanced, integrated, and coherent—not perfect. In contrast, an overly rigid handwriting reveals excessive control, which means the ego is dominated by a **too-strong *superego***. In further contrast, when the ***id*** dominates, the writing displays marked variability and a lack of consistency, pointing to poor impulse control.

The term **ego *drive*** refers to the writer's core emotional motivations—the inner needs that come from the id and propel them toward action and achievement. **Ego *strength***, on the other hand, describes the ego's capacity to manage these inner drives and the moral constraints of the superego in a constructive way. A writer with good ego strength is able to meet their needs without causing harm to themselves or others.

Strong form within a good gestalt reflects in a secure, well-developed, self-confident ego. The writer demonstrates the ability to balance his wants and needs, exercising foresight and planning to achieve satisfaction at the appropriate time. He is the driver, not the passenger—in control of his direction and choices.

Weak Gestalt, Weak Ego

By contrast, a *weak* or *disturbed* gestalt suggests a poorly developed or unstable ego, which signals broader difficulties in day-to-day functioning. Further analysis is required to determine whether the disturbance also involves the superego (intellectual/moral area), the id (impulse/action area), or both.

- *When the gestalt is negative due to weak or disturbed **form**, the problem is with the ego.*
- *When the gestalt is negative due to a weak or disturbed **spatial arrangement**, the problem is with the way the writer thinks (perspective).*
- *When due to weak or disturbed **movement** (discussed in Part 3), the problem is with the basic driving force.*

102

A newborn baby does not arrive in the world with a fully formed ego. Instead, the ego gradually develops over time as the infant begins to understand that he is separate and distinct from his environment. By around age three, having made the remarkable discovery that he can cause things to happen; that he does not have to passively wait until things happen to him, a typically developing child begins testing his autonomy.

Ego is the Self, as separate from others

Ideally, the child is nurtured by loving caregivers who support this emerging sense of self and encourage growth toward independence and responsibility. This development journey is reflected in handwriting. The handwriting of a person with a healthy ego won't appear 'perfect'—nor should it. Rather, it reflects the unique ways the writer has responded to both positive and negative life experiences.

Abuse and the Development of Form

When the ego is allowed to develop in a healthy way, it lays the foundation for an adult who is equipped to lead a successful, balanced life. But what happens when a child is neglected or abused, or—at the other end of the spectrum—overprotected, which is an overlooked form of abuse? In such cases, the ego may not develop properly, and the effects are frequently visible the handwriting.

Signs of poor ego development include *weak* or *disturbed form, disordered spatial arrangement,* and/or *disturbed movement* (movement is covered in Part 3). These disturbances contribute to a poor gestalt—an overall handwriting impression that reflects inner dysfunction.

When all three of these foundational elements—the big pictures of space, form, and movement—are compromised, the writer is apt to experience significant difficulty coping with everyday life.

Psychology teaches us that behavior arises from the complex interplay of *nature* (inborn personality traits) and *nurture* (environmental influences). A child who is neglected or abused may grow up emotionally withdrawn, having learned that vulnerability—such as expressing love—is unsafe. Alternatively, such a child may develop aggressive, antisocial behavior. Although seemingly sheltered from harm, the overprotected child may grow up overly dependent, lacking the self-confidence to function independently.

Emotional Development In Handwriting

In the *emotionally withdrawn* person, we see wide spacing between letters and/or words, symbolizing both inner and outer emotional distance, and as we have seen earlier, margins mirror one's attitude toward past and future. The form is also affected. When simplified, the handwriting may appear stripped-down or linear, with minimal ornamentation and few loops. Since loops serve as containers for emotion, their absence speaks to a rejection or suppression of emotional expression.

The *aggressive, antisocial* personality on the other hand—explored in depth in my book on personality disorders—leaves a distinct imprint on handwriting. The aggressive or antisocial person often adopts angular writing, often along with heavy pressure. The angle is a forceful and sharp form, suggesting inner tension, hostility, or control through dominance.

For the *dependent* personality, the picture of space is typically crowded, signaling a lack of psychological boundaries and a strong need for closeness or reassurance. The form either resembles copybook style or is overly rounded, with soft shapes indicating passivity and a reliance on external support.

---

*Handwriting with a disturbed form and/or movement **but also has a strong picture of space** suggests that the writer is able to use his organizational skills to help him function reasonably well in important areas of his life.*

Persona Writing: When the Mask Becomes the Message

Everyone wears different "masks" in daily life—social roles or personas adapted to various environments. One individual may project an outgoing image in public while feeling shy or insecure inside. Another might display an authoritarian attitude at work, yet be a pussycat at home. Still another may appear charming to outsiders, yet behave abusively to their family behind closed doors.

In handwriting, these masks become visible in the *form* a writer adopts. But perhaps even more telling than the style itself is whether the form is *natural* or *contrived*. When handwriting looks beautiful but appears *drawn* rather than natural and spontaneous, we call this ***persona writing***.

As illustrated here in a sample written by author Dominick Dunne, rather than looking natural, the handwriting acquires an artistic or overly stylized appearance that draws attention to itself.

Persona writing may be ornate, controlled, or unusually perfect—so its embellishments cause it to resemble a crafted image—a mask. The projected self overshadows the genuine self. The personality we see on the page is a constructed façade, and the deeper, authentic self is obscured, hidden beneath layers of performance and self-preservation.

Like this artwork, persona writing is stylized, with more contraction (control) than release (contraction/ release is part of rhythm, covered in Part 3). For the persona writer, appearance—form—is more important than the substance of the message. The focus is on creating an impression, not an authentic expression or communication.

Those close to such a person may ask themselves a lingering question: *is the charm genuine and sincere, or is it just for show?*

The persona writer has a deep, unconscious need to be seen as perfect, a drive that permeates many aspects of their life. Considerable time and energy may be devoted to cultivating an idealized image—personal appearance, social presentation, and even the home environment. That home may resemble a museum more than a lived-in space, reflecting order, beauty, and control—not necessarily the kind of warmth where people live and enjoy life.

At its core, this need for perfection is rooted in insecurity and accompanied by a powerful need to maintain control. The writer lives with an internal fear: if they relax control, even for a moment, chaos will erupt and disaster will reign. So, the carefully managed image becomes a defense mechanism, a shield against inner disorder and perceived external threat.

Stylized Handwriting: When Aesthetics Overrides Expression

Further along the spectrum of control is a kind of stylized handwriting that carries an even more artificial quality than persona. It reveals a layer of social polish and sophistication, yet tends to appear lifeless—static on the page. The writer's behavior mirrors this artificiality: polished, composed, but lacking emotional spontaneity.

106

Stylized handwriting overlaps with persona writing, but there are subtle differences. As seen in the earlier sample of Dominick Dunne, persona writing often reveals an artistic inclination—carefully crafted yet still retaining some emotional tone. What defines it as **persona** is the high degree of regularity as a dominant feature, and the emphasis of form over feeling, which diminishes the naturalness.

Stylized handwriting, by contrast, is even less natural. The form dominates the movement to an even greater degree. Like a beautiful but static piece of artwork, the writing may be visually striking, yet lack the dynamic liveliness that contributes to a healthy gestalt. The writer holds in mind a clear idea of what constitutes "beautiful" look, and carefully constructs it to meet that idea. Aesthetics are paramount.

This next handwriting, by a ballerina, is a fascinating combination of simplified forms and elaboration that disturb the gestalt. And yet, the high-flying t's in this elegant writing cause the viewer to imagine her leaping into the air in a *grand jetè* or *pirouette*.

The sample below was written by an accomplished and charming defense attorney. Clearly, she put thought and effort into shaping these original forms, writing them with care. The spatial layout is precise and controlled, but there is little movement in the writing, which disturbs the form. The writing lacks direction—it doesn't venture outward but instead stays within a self-imposed safe zone.

I was born in New York in 1951. My older brother, Jeff was two and was always my hero. We moved to Detroit, then California where my brother, Jon was born... Jon is a doll, I wish I liked his wife. We moved to New Jersey, back to California, back to New Jersey and then to Ohio. In 1972 I met a fascinating man who I married the very next week. If I had eighty five more pages, I'd tell you some terrific stories!

The writer places high esteem on appearances. She is deliberate in how she presents herself and showing anything less than perfection—by her own internal standards—feels humiliating. Even her capital letters, though printed, are stylish and carefully rendered, as are several lower case letter forms.

She reveals very little of her true self, keeping vulnerability hidden behind her carefully constructed image. As a personal side note: she was willing to "embellish" the truth, or fabricate an elaborate story that suited her aims or might be helpful to a client.

What matters more than whether the gestalt is weak or actively disturbed is the clear signal that something is out of balance—something that needs to be 'fixed'—the visual harmony is disrupted, and to restore it, the elaborations would need to be reduced or removed.

When Embellishment Masks Insecurity

Progressing further along the spectrum is the handwriting where the writer uses excessive embellishment as a psychological defense. This need to attract attention stems from deep feelings of inadequacy. The result is writing that produces either a weak or disturbed gestalt.

One who exaggerates their handwriting tends to be an exaggerator in life as well. Their home may be overdecorated, crammed with collections and ornate items. Their stories are likely to be filled with colorful details—many of which may be inaccurate or entirely fabricated.

This pattern reveals insecurity and inner conflict. The more embellished and elaborate the writing, the more difficulty the writer has in seeing things objectively. His judgment becomes clouded and subjective, and his thinking unnecessarily complicated. Emotionally, he is prone to making mountains out of molehills, responding to relatively minor events with disproportionate intensity.

Note, however, despite inner emotional turbulence, as in the sample above, the writer can be highly successful in their public life. Elizabeth Dole was the wife of Vice President Bob Dole and president of the American Red Cross from 1991-1999. She is an attorney, author, and politician.

Elaborate handwriting lies farther along the spectrum from stylized or persona handwriting, differing both in degree and taste.

While **stylized** writing may still reflect aesthetic control, **elaboration** introduces excess and complication. A style marked by added embellishments results in unnecessary or overly complex movements. Common features include ornate or decorated capital letters, decorative signatures, hooks and other decorations inside oval letters.

As in the sample below, there may be curled, circular strokes where they don't belong—in this case manifesting as loops and swirls, or there might be ballooning upper or lower loops that distort the writing's natural rhythm and interfere with its readability.

These excessive flourishes indicate not just a visual preference, but an emotional pattern: a need to stand out, to distract, or to compensate for deeper psychological insecurities.

110

Elaborations can take many different forms. At first glance, the writing above seems to be more 'normal.' As you look closer, however, you see many elaborate forms, especially in the "Greek E's", which don't quite fit.

In the next two samples, the crowded appearance and excessive ornamentation, combined with the crowded (weak) spatial arrangement, immediately draws the eye and disturbs the gestalt. These writings have weak form and spatial arrangements.

Sample 1

I would like to inform you that 26812 Claudette St. unit #309 is available for lease if any of your friends or relatives are interested in moving into our neighborhood, please have them call me.

Washer and Dryer are included and Owner will allow pets on a Case to Case.

I look forward to hearing from you.

From my early years to the present time in my life I have been blessed by "God." Wonderful parents, and a family that supported my every need. I have found that life is blessed if you follow your heart and dreams.

111

Sample 3 shows obvious and extreme over-elaboration. The long rightward strokes that cover up much of the writing detract from legibility. Considering this is the address on an envelope, it's puzzling that the writer would use this form.

At the opposite end of the spectrum is the highly simplified, intelligent writing of naturalist Jane Goodall. Which you saw earlier in the text. This is a good example of strong form, as well as a strong spatial arrangement.

Jane Goodall

112

Lesson Nine
Connective Forms

The term *connective form* refers to the ligatures that link one letter to the next. More than simply connectors, these forms also describe the shapes of the letters themselves—and each shape offers insight into the personality of the writer who habitually uses it.

In this section, we will examine the basic curved and linear shapes that are themselves the underpinnings of form and the foundation of handwriting structure. Previously, we discussed form a comprising the *figure* in writing. We talked about the continuum from copybook, simplified, printing, persona, stylized, embellished—and considered how form manifests from strong to weak to disturbed. Next we turn to the four major types of *connective forms* and letter shapes:

Ties That Bind

- *Garland – One of the two curved forms; a soft, curved shape that is open at the bottom, resembling a cup or a U.*

- *Arcade — the second of the two curved forms; an inverted curved shape that opens at the top, resembling an arch or an upside down U.*

- *Angle — sharp, straight stroke forms with abrupt transitions.*

- *Thread — a loosely connected, often poorly defined line that thins out. Think of a cat playing with a ball of yarn.*

Each form carries psychological significance. Writers who rely on a single connective form in their writing relate best to their own personality type, and often have trouble understanding motivations and needs different from their own. The well-integrated writer, on the other hand, uses a combination of forms, though one may be dominant.

In the sections ahead, we'll explore the characteristics, meanings, and implications of each form, and what they reveal about the inner life of the writer.

Rounded Forms - Garlands

The term **garland** traditionally refers to a circular band of foliage or flowers used for decoration. While this floral definition may seem unrelated to handwriting, it's the circular aspect that makes it relevant. In handwriting analysis, a garland is the *lower half* of a circle—cup-shaped—open and receptive. When most letter connections curve upward from the baseline, forming this cup-like shape, this is a garland writer.

Garland writing is most easily observed in letters such as m, n, and u, where the connecting strokes are curved on the bottom. In the handwriting below, for example, you may notice that the ms and ns form open-bottom loops. These are classic garland forms. In the same sample, the th and so combinations display garland forms—open on top—indicating a blend of connective styles.

The sample above is used with permission of Jens Windeleff from his excellent book, *C.G. Jung and the Circle Around Him,* which examines their handwriting.

As mentioned earlier, curved, or rounded shapes in handwriting suggest traits that are stereotypically associated with femininity—regardless of the writer's gender. These traits include softness, tact, nurturing, a desire to take care of others, emotional expression, a need for connection.

114

In a positive gestalt—balanced and harmonious—particularly when blended with other forms, there is flexibility, cooperation, and emotional accessibility.

Variations of the Garland Form

In a *negative* gestalt—unbalanced and inharmonious—especially when garlands dominate to the *exclusion* of other forms—or the garlands are shallow or weak—these same shapes may indicate excessive compliance, over-accommodation, or emotional dependence. In such cases, the writer may be too eager to please or may struggle with assertiveness, appearing to be a pushover.

While garland connections typically suggest openness and sociability, some forms—though not common—evolve into exaggerated or uncommon variants.

Clothesline or Flat Garland

This variation gets its name from its low, flat appearance—it "creeps" along the baseline like laundry strung out to dry. The effect is a series of flattened, shallow cups. This form depicts a superficial friendliness: the writer appears pleasant on the surface but lacks depth in relationships and may be a back-stabber. Here are two examples.

Clothesline Garland

115

Deep Garland

True to its name, this form is marked by pronounced, deep cup shapes. It reflects the writer is excessively open to outside experiences, often to the point of overwhelm. There is difficulty asserting boundaries—the wide, deep form reach out and encroach on others' space—but with a big smile. In this style, the m and n closely resemble w and u. Think of a cup so open it overflows. Sincerity may be lacking.

The next sample, a man's garland handwriting, is a good example of how handwriting does not reliably reveal gender.

Double Bow

This unusual connective form combines elements of both garland and arcade, creating a figure that resembles two overlapping curves—like a lowercase m formed from both cup and arch. Writers who use this form struggle with

116

decision-making. Just like their handwriting can't settle on one shape, they find it hard to commit to a choice. Either he can't make up his mind, or may easily change it under pressure. It's not easy to find a sample of this form.

On the positive side, the double bow form reflects imagination and creative potential, often found in those think outside the box and approach problems with originality.

Rounded Forms - Arcades

The term *arcade* refers to a structure composed of a series of arches supported by columns—forms that are strong, structured, and protective. In handwriting, the arcade is the visual opposite of the garland: it is curved on the top and open on the bottom. This creates a closed form—symbolically and psychologically—indicating a writer who is less receptive to outside influence and is more inwardly focused.

Where the garland suggests openness and emotional accessibility, the arcade conveys reserve and self-containment. The arch provide structure and support, a place of protection. Writers who favor arcade forms may share the emotional qualities of garland writers, but they express it less openly.

The closed arch structure suggests a need to protect the ego, to maintain personal boundaries and shut out what they view as intrusion by others. Some types of arcades reveal a secretive, emotionally closed-off, guarded person.

The Role of Speed in Arcades

Like all connective forms, the interpretation of arcades depends significantly on writing speed. The meaning of arcades in a slow handwriting will be negative, and in a faster writing, more positive.

- *Fast arcades in a positive gestalt point to quick, original thinking. The writer jumps from one idea to the next, offering creative or unusual solutions to problems. They may also display aesthetic sensibilities or interest in fields like art or architecture.*

- *Slow arcades often reflect a more problematic personality pattern. Unless they are produced by a writer of limited intellect, often are a primary indicator for premeditated dishonesty, calculated behavior, and a high level of emotional inhibition. A writer who consistently uses slow, deliberate arcades is motivated by a desire to conceal true feelings or intentions.*

117

Interpreting Excessive Circularity

A handwriting comprised of repetitive cup-like curves can resemble little open mouths, symbolically waiting to be fed. This visual metaphor—excessively rounded handwriting—reflects an emotional hunger, rooted in early unmet needs.

When a handwriting sample at first glance appears circular (too rounded), whether due to excessive garlands or arcades—it is an extreme.

Writers who display this exaggerated roundness in adulthood unconsciously seek to compensate for what they lacked through oral indulgences such as:

- *Overeating*
- *Smoking or excessive drinking*
- *Constant talking*
- *Chewing gum or toothpicks*

These behaviors are subconscious efforts to fill emotional voids that trace back to childhood deprivation, whether real or perceived.

---

*Look at the m's and n's
Open on the top = garland
Rounded on top = arcade.*

The following handwriting sample is that of Nicole Brown Simpson, ex-wife of football star, OJ Simpson, who was acquitted of killing her and her friend. This is a good example of an excessively rounded form, which is mainly made up of arcades. The overall gestalt is weak, primarily due to the crowded spatial arrangement, which leaves little room for clarity or perspective. The lack of spacing between words suggests a tendency to act impulsively, without adequate pre-planning. The form is similarly weak, characterized by unoriginal, excessively rounded letters.

These arcade shapes, while deviating somewhat from the copybook standard, do not enhance the individuality of the script. Instead, they diminish its strength and point to underdeveloped ego structure.

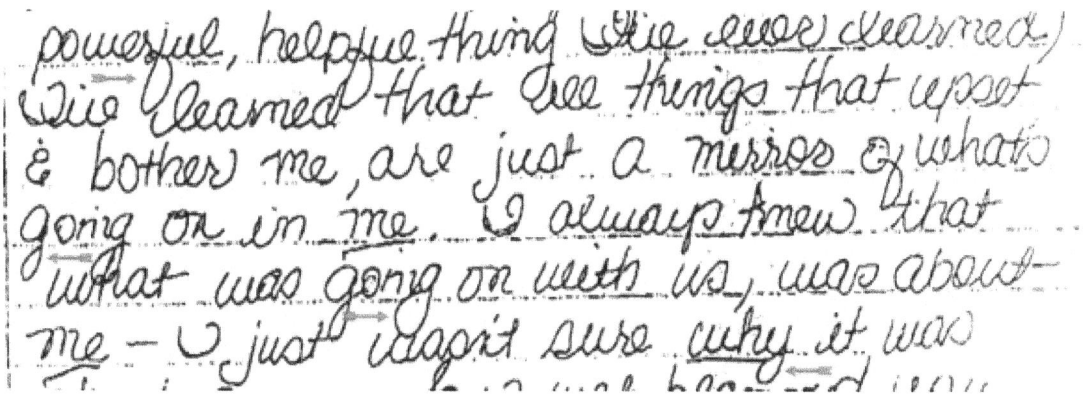

Nicole Brown Simpson

This combination of poor spatial organization and compromised form signals a writer who struggles with boundaries, self-definition, and emotional self-regulation. It's sadly typical of many women who get into abusive situations and find it difficult to extract themselves

Angle Connective Form

An angle is defined as the space formed where two lines or planes intersect.

In handwriting, when one straight stroke joins another at a sharp point, it creates an angular connection. This form contrasts strongly with the softness of garlands and the rounded arches of arcades.

Angular connections are traditionally associated with stereotypically masculine traits—regardless of the writer's gender. These included qualities such as:

- *Toughness*
- *Aggression*
- *Dominance*
- *Independence*
- *Competitiveness*
- *Ambition*
- *Authority and discipline*
- *Decisiveness*

Think of the triangle, the strongest geometric structure known. It cannot be easily broken or collapsed, and this symbolic strength is embedded in the angular form. The straight line—the shortest distance between two points and a symbol of strength represents directness and clarity. This is the philosophy of the angle writer: no frills, no flourishes, just get to the point. Small talk is of little interest.

Writers who favor angle forms prefer efficiency and decisiveness, both in thought and action. Their bluntness may be interpreted as assertiveness, or, in a negative gestalt, as insensitivity or hostility.

Following are three examples of how angles may appear in different types of handwriting. Review these samples and consider:

- *How do the angle forms influence your impression of the writer's personality?*
- *In what ways might these angular traits be expressed in the writer's daily life, work, or relationships?*

120

The writer with many angles has a critical nature and may be difficult to live with. However, the inclusion of some curved forms slightly can soften the overall impression. The rounded strokes temper the angularity and allow for some of the more positive traits associated with angles, such as strength, directness, and decisiveness, without tipping into emotional volatility.

Balance of Curves/Straight Lines

When used in balance with curved forms, angles provide strength and structure to handwriting. Combined with curved forms, angles contribute to a harmonious, visually pleasing picture—a good gestalt. The contrast between soft and linear strokes reflects psychological flexibility: the ability to be assertive when needed, yet receptive and adaptable in relationships.

However, when the writing becomes *dominated* by angles and straight strokes, especially when combined with *heavy pressure* (pressure is discussed in Part 3), it raises psychological red flags.

Excessive angularity produces tension and signals internal conflict, frustration, and repressed aggression. The energy buildup may result in sudden, dramatic emotional outbursts that, when released, can produce a frightening explosion, as was seen in the writer of the next highly angular sample, that of Robert "Bobby Joe" Long, a serial rapist and murderer who was executed in Florida in 2019.

121

Case Example: Bobby Joe Long

Long's handwriting displays extreme aggression, evidenced by slashing, angular strokes and intense pressure. Long's angular forms are tight, like a coiled spring, contributing to the disturbed gestalt. The writing visually communicates an intense inner pressure and a potential for violent discharge.

Long's printed writing, seen below, was quite different, and hides much of his true personality. However, the small size, angled lower zones, and lack of release are red flags for pathology

122

Thread Forms

The final connective form in our discussion isn't truly a form at all, hence the name '*thread.*' A thread is defined as a long thin line of material—such as light smoke or fiber. In handwriting, thready forms appear as a thin, often illegible line formed by a breakdown of traditional letter forms.

In some cases, the writer's thoughts and hand are moving so rapidly that there is no time to form complete, well-defined letters. The writing becomes abbreviated, resembling shorthand, with just enough shape to trigger recognition. Thread writers are quick thinkers, mentally agile, and impatient with formalities or details.

In other cases, the writer is deliberately evasive, attempting to obscure their meaning by omitting or breaking down letter forms so that the reader can't be sure of exactly what it's supposed to say. This provides plausible deniability. If questioned later, the writer can protest, "But that's not what I meant." It allows room for a reinterpretation or retreat, a psychological defense against accountability.

The difference may be found in the two types of thread:
primary and secondary.

Primary vs. Secondary Thread

Thread forms are particularly important to analyze in the context of intent. Are they the result of mental quickness, or emotional avoidance? As always, interpretation depends on the surrounding elements and the overall gestalt.

Thread in handwriting is the result of a breakdown in form—but not all thread is equal. It is crucial to distinguish between primary and secondary thread when evaluating this feature in context.

Primary Thread

- ***Primary thread** is made with firm pressure, typically seen at the ends of words and within some letters in a fast, fluid handwriting.*
- *Though forms are abbreviated, they are often still **recognizable**.*
- *This style reflects mental quickness, high intelligence, and an efficient, no-frills approach to communication.*

123

When supported by a strong spatial arrangement,
primary thread contributes to a strong, positive gestalt.

Example: This sample written by actor **Hugh Grant** demonstrates primary thread combined with some angular forms in a strongly simplified and intelligent script. The thread is made with pressure and control in a strong spatial arrangement, producing a crisp, purposeful writing style in a good gestalt.

Grant himself has often referred to himself as being grumpy, which in his handwriting looks like impatience, seen in the greatly simplified, abbreviated forms and lack of right trend.

Another example of primary thread appears below. Many of the letters thin out but are still quite legible. This sample is obviously very different from Hugh Grant's, and while impatience may still be seen in the speed, it is manifested in different ways.

124

Secondary Thread

Secondary thread is more problematic. Truly formless, when seen mid-word, letters disintegrate into indistinct, illegible strokes.

- *These forms lack structure, coherence, and clarity in communication.*
- *Since the purpose of writing is to communicate, such illegibility may reflect a hostile attitude, whether conscious or unconscious.*
- *When secondary thread dominates in a poor gestalt in likely indicates emotional instability or psychological overwhelm. In such cases, it's best to obtain additional information about the writer.*

Case Example: This sample has a disturbed gestalt marked by deteriorated form, chaotic spacing, and degraded movement. The letter forms have disintegrated and are so indefinite as to be barely legible. The writing appears strung out and nearly illegible. This is a red flag for internal pressure so intense that it may point to a person on the verge of emotional collapse. The writer feels so pressured by daily life that he can barely function. Mental illness may play a part.

Balanced forms

The most desirable handwriting shows a balanced combination of connective forms—garland, arcade, angle, and some thread. This reflects psychological flexibility, emotional maturity, and the ability to adapt to situations and interpersonal demands.

Important reminder: balance does not mean perfect.

In virtually every sample—even in otherwise well-integrated handwriting—there will be features that might be improved.

Example: in this sample, some long, curved initial and final strokes add an element of elaboration, and the writing is crowded for the amount of space used. Though subtle, these flourishes detract the visual harmony of the writing. Such embellishments suggest a need for attention, dramatization, or an overconcern with impression.

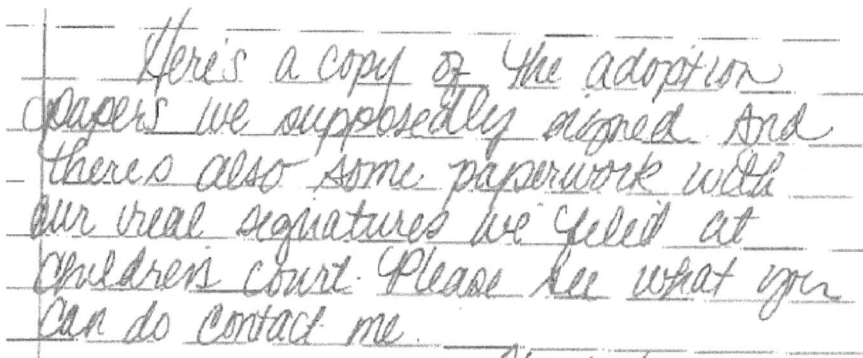

In interpretation, always weigh these details in the context of the handwriting you are analyzing. A writing can still reflect a well-adjusted personality even when it includes small deviations from ideal form—as long as the overall balance is preserved.

Next are some reasonably well-balanced samples in a good gestalt.

126

[Handwritten text:] The Complete Idiot's Guide to Handwriting Analysis will make an excellent additio to an already spectacular series. I can wait to get my hands on a copy of this book.

[Handwritten text:] meet with him to discuss breakThrough proposal. Joe Williams had forwarded Dealer, Stocking Distributor and master distributor Price lists to WIZHMAN

Following are examples of different connective forms. See if you can figure out which is which, starting with a letter former President Richard Nixon to newsman Ted Koppel, and continuing to some 'regular folk.'

[Handwritten text:] Dear Ted — Because I will be vacationing with the family in the Caribbean — I will be unable to attend the reception commemorating the fifth anniversary of Nightline

Richard Nixon

1

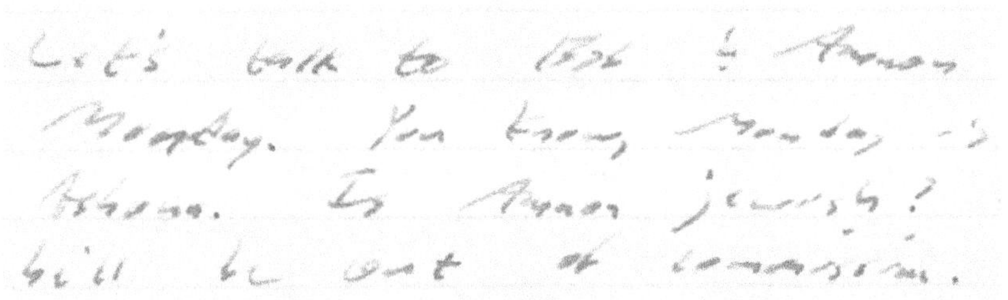
Let's talk to Bob & Aaron
Monday. You know, Monday is
Aaron. Is Aaron jewish?
Will be out of commission.

What connective form is this?

What about the form above? The ones below

2

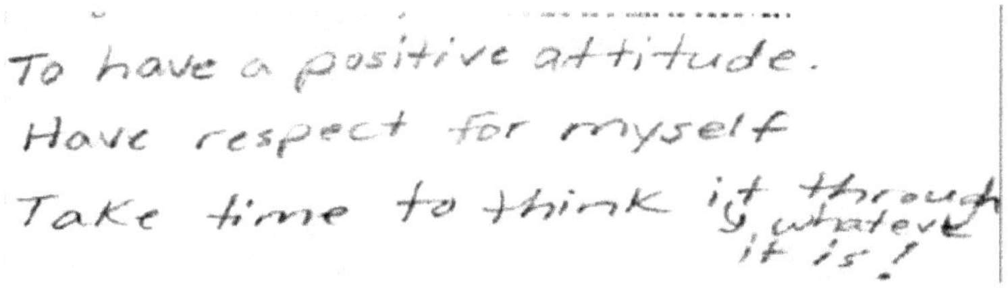
To have a positive attitude.
Have respect for myself
Take time to think it through, whatever it is!

3

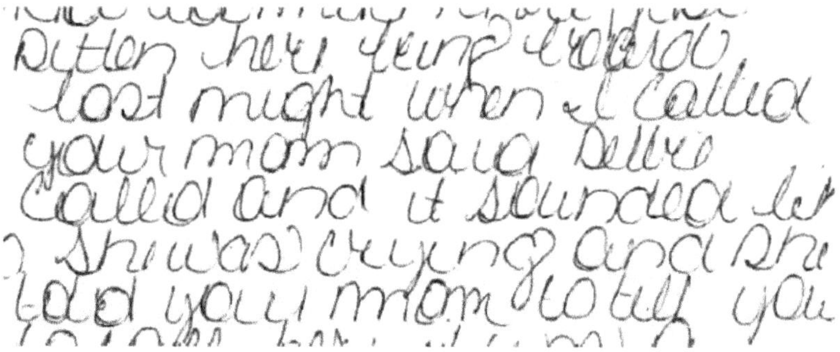
Dillon here
last night when I called
your mom said Debbie
called and it sounded like
she was crying and she
told your mom to tell you

4

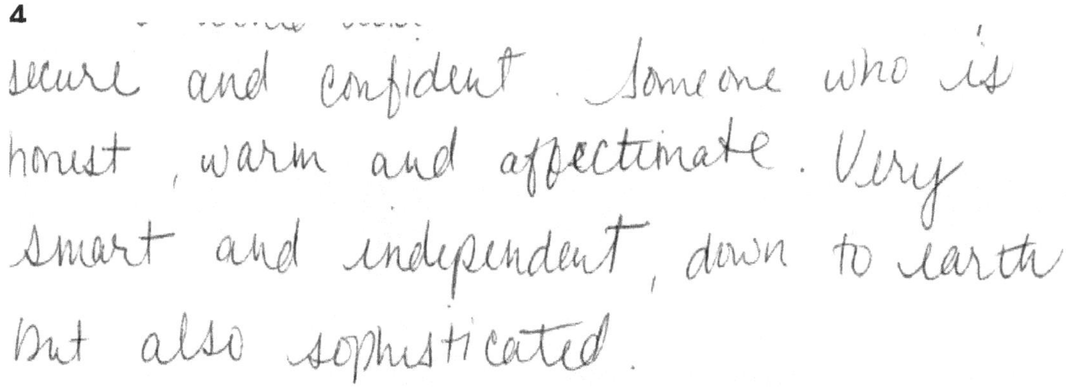
secure and confident. Someone who is
honest, warm and affectimate. Very
smart and independent, down to earth
but also sophisticated.

Lesson Ten
Printed Writing

Handwriting analysts trained in the trait-stroke method often express concern when faced with printed handwriting, which was not always part of the curriculum. Traditional stroke names and trait identifiers do not easily apply. If you've shared that concern, take comfort: printing is writing, too, and with the gestalt method, it can be analyzed just as effectively as cursive. As you will see, the gestalt method allows you to analyze any type of graphic expression in any language or form.

Gestalt principles apply to all writing styles

Printing as a Response to Trauma

In cursive writing, ligatures (connections between letters) symbolize the writer's need for interpersonal connection. Printers, by definition, cut off these ligatures. On a symbolic level, this habit reveals a tendency to disconnect emotionally, breaking off emotional, if not physical, connections to others, even when the writer is outwardly sociable.

In many cases, habitual printers adopt that style as a result of a painful or traumatic precipitating event or series of events. These might include:

— *Childhood loss or abandonment that left the writer afraid to be close to anyone.*

— *Frequent relocation, e.g., military families who moved around from school to school without establishing a stable home.*

— *Periods of being unhoused, with no opportunity to put down roots.*

— *Trauma, such as the death of a loved one o pet.*

— *Divorce or instability at home.*

129

Connectedness and Emotional Availability

Particularly when it becomes the exclusive style the writer uses, printing can be a defensive adaptation. Breaking all or most of the connections between the letters (and with other people) feels safer. The whispers to an unconscious message to themselves: *"If you don't get too close to others, it won't hurt as much when they leave."*

Context Matters

Some work requires printing—first responders, law enforcement officers, architects, engineers, etc. These individuals may use a more connected writing style in their personal lives. When available, a personal sample is preferred for analysis. However, if only printing is available, then that is a valid reflection of their personality at the time of writing.

Printers whose letters touch or nearly touch want to make connections, while still holding back.

Types of Printed Writing

Just as in cursive writing, there are several common forms of printing:

- *Manuscript printing*: Combines upper and lower case letters; common to people who never learned cursive. Often used for clarity and may reflect a need for control or formality. Less formality, more friendly than block printers.

- *Block printing*: All capital letters with no upper or lower zones. Emotionally guarded, gaining trust takes time and patience—like peeling an onion, revealing emotional layers slowly, over a long period of time. Even though the writer may not admit it themselves, their partner's response will usually be a knowing nod. Block printers are typically self-reliant, somewhat egocentric, and the center of their own world. there is no strong need for approval. Associated with emotional distance, formality, or a desire to conceal vulnerability.

Printscript

- **Printscript**: *A blend of printing and cursive. When integrated into a **good gestalt**, this hybrid form can be a sign of creativity, flexibility, and cognitive dexterity. In a **weak** or **disturbed gestalt**, it's more likely about attracting attention, inconsistency, or erratic emotional expression. Impulsivity, impatience, and a lack of consistency.*

Each of these printed forms has its variations and subtypes, some of which will be illustrated at the end of this section. As in any other writing style, there are far too many to show them all.

Analyzing printing

One of the great strengths of the gestalt approach lies in its adaptability. You are learning to observe *how* something is written, not just what it *looks like*. Whether cursive, printing, or a hybrid, every sample reveals personality through its spatial arrangement, form, and movement

And, just like cursive writing, printed writing has a spatial arrangement that includes

- *Margins,*
- *Baseline*
- *Word, letter, and line spacing*
- *Form (figure)*
- *Rhythm and movement.*

These are the building blocks of any graphic expression and can be analyzed regardless of language or writing system. Whether the script is written in English, Hebrew, or any other alphabet, the overall pattern—the gestalt—will fall into one of three categories you have been studying: strong, weak, or disturbed. If the gestalt is negative (weak or disturbed), you can further examine the pictures of space, form, and movement to pinpoint the area(s) of concern.

Applying the principles you've been developing in the first half of the course, you can analyze printed handwriting in the same way you analyze cursive.

Ultimately, printing, like any other writing style, must be analyzed in totality. Focus on the whole before the parts, and interpret the individual features only in the context of the full writing sample. Following are several printed samples for practice.

YOUNG THINKING, EN
CREATIVE, SELF MOTIVATE,
SUCCESSFUL IN HER OWN R
— ATTRACTIVE — A WIZZ
THE Best!

Trying to learn meditation, I felt
really cloudy this morning. I tried
to meditate but couldn't connect. I'm
moving soon, I think the stress about
finding a place was the issue today.
I went to the gym, felt very
empowered and centered after my

NJOYED HAVING THE OPPORTUNIT
YOU AS WELL AS HAVING YOU
I FOUND YOUR CONVERSATION
EDGE OF YOUR HANDWRITING AN
NTERESTING. THANKS FOR COM

What I am looking for is very simple.
I'm looking for a person who has a fulfilling
career and whose life is very active. I know
that I have the same sort of life. In that
context, I want someone who can share
what they are doing and what they feel

I am inspired to learn... pretty much
anything that is new to me. particularly
as it relates somewhat technically

YOUR LATEST NEWSLETTER IS
FANTASTIC AS ALWAYS I ESPECIALLY LIKED
THE ARTICLE ABOUT BREAKING INTO JURY
SCREENING. ALSO "INSTRUCTIONS FOR LIFE"

DESIGN IS WHAT MAKES
THE MUNDANE BEAUTIFUL.
. THE PEOPLE WHO CHOOSE
WELL INSPIRE ME. THEY
KNOW WHAT IS WORTH SPENDING
TIME ON.

eans that formed on ea
tus hyphothesis was testi
tested experimentally, when
scientists, Stanley Miller a
d Oparins theory by stin
ons of early earth in th

I am looking for a special woman in
serious Relationship to have deep (
Polite, truthful, understanding, thou
Passionate, Caring, Romantic, outgoin
distinguished, Reliable partner, wit
humor. She also would have o,

The natural beauty of the Swiss Alps
inspire me. The spectacular mountains
and glaciers, the wildflowers; the
pristine air and bracing temperatures
contrasted with warming sun... it

passions and are true to
themselves really inspire me
Being able to trust in your
own instincts so much and not
be swayed by the masses is a
difficult thing to do & I thin

134

PART THREE
Movement

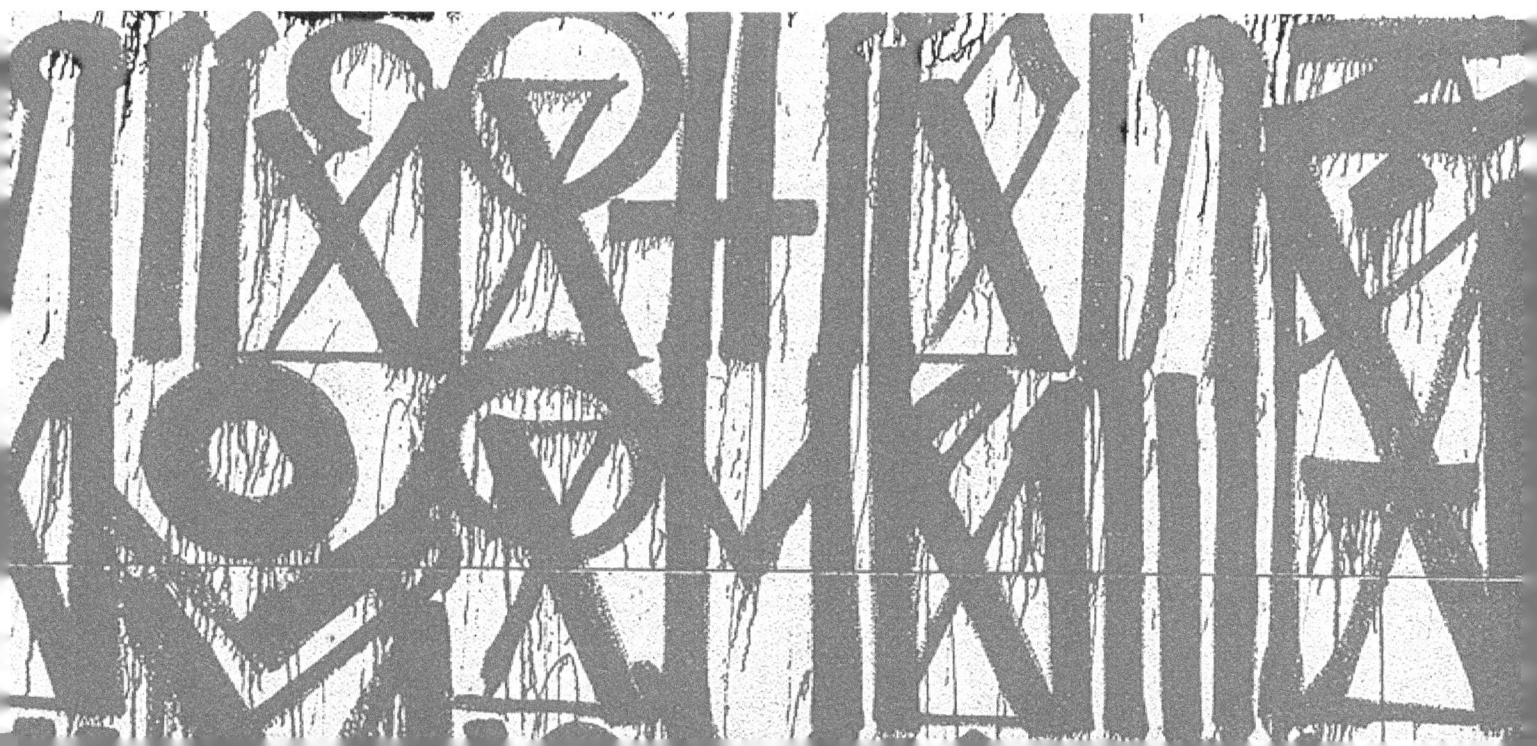

Lesson Eleven
Introduction to Movement

We have reached the most complex aspect of handwriting: *movement*. To the untrained eye, handwriting may appear as a static line on the page, but in truth, it is the visible trace of human dynamic action. Without movement, handwriting would amount to nothing more than a dot of ink on the paper.

Einstein said: *"Nothing happens until something moves."*

Movement is not just a technical feature of handwriting, it is a window into vitality and motivation. It shows us how the writer engages with life: directly or evasively, fluidly, or awkwardly, with confidence or restraint.

Space, form, and movement are an inseparable triad. Although **movement** is just one of these three essential components of handwriting, it is the force that **creates form**, and both are influenced by their relationship to **space**.

Of these three, movement may be the most significant in shaping the overall gestalt, as it leaves the strongest visual cues.

The moment the writer's hand begins to propel the pen across the page, it initiates a dynamic trail of ink. Ultimately, it is **movement** that breathes life into handwriting—creating form within the frame of the available space and shaping the personality of the writing as a whole. It is the essence of expression, operating on multiple levels.

137

Handwriting is Multidimensional

At first glance, a flat sheet of paper may appear to represent only a single dimension. But when we look closer, we find that what is written on it occupies multiple dimensions, each one contributing to the expressive power of the written word.

In analyzing movement, we examine how often the hand stops and starts, the degree of pressure applied to the paper, the upward lift of the pen and its trace in the air before alighting again; the pace with which it traverses the writing surface; the type of rhythm it produces. These movements directly influence the figure/ground relationship that we have explored in previous lessons.

By definition, *dimension* refers to a measurable extent—of space, magnitude, or scope. In handwriting, these dimensions unfold through the movement of the hand:

1. **Movement across the page**—from left to right in Roman languages such as English (or right to left in languages like Hebrew or Arabic)—constitutes the first dimension.
2. **Vertical movement**, creating upper and lower extensions of the letters, gives us the second dimension—up and down.
3. **Depth, or pressure** into the paper is the third dimension. It reflects how delicately or forcefully the pen meets the writing surface.
4. **Air strokes**—movements that occur above the page, as the pen lifts and re-positions before returning to the writing surface—represents the fourth dimension.

These four types of movement give handwriting its dynamic, living quality, far beyond static lines of ink.

While spatial arrangement refers to the *layout* of writing on the page, and form refers to its *stylistic* appearance— the way the writing looks—it is *movement* that draws the eye and lets us sense how well balanced the writing is and whether it has a good gestalt.

138

Definitions of Movement:

- **To change in position from one point to another**
  - *In handwriting, movement physically takes the pen from one point on the page to another*

- **To progress in sequence; go forward or backward**
  - *Although writing typically moves forward, effective handwriting must flow in all directions—consider the circular motion in letters like o or e.*

- **To follow a specified course**
  - *The path of movement is guided by form—original copybook patterns as well as any individual modifications the writer introduces.*

- **To start off; depart**
  - *Until the pen moves, nothing exists but a dot on the page. That first movement represents the departure point of expression.*

- **To be put in motion or to turn according to a prescribed motion**
  - *The style and rhythm of the writer's movement reflects energy levels and personal drive.*

- **To be active in a particular environment**
  - *Handwriting movement reflects the writer's activity level and engagement with their inner and outer environment.*

Strong/Weak/Disturbed

Just as we have categorized space and form, *movement* in handwriting is also classified as strong, weak, or disturbed, each of which reveals something essential about the writer's inner state and outward behavior.

- *Strong* movement is fluid, confident, and purposeful. It shows well-directed energy and psychological strength.

- *Weak* movement is hesitant or erratic, often indicating low vitality, lack of conviction, or internal conflict.

- *Disturbed* movement appears chaotic or forced, suggesting emotional turmoil, impulsiveness, or poor self-regulation.

Each of these categories affects the gestalt and must be interpreted within the larger context of space and form.

139

Movement Mirrors Life

There are as many different types of movement in handwriting as there are in life. To understand this, try a simple observation exercise: sit in a busy public place and watch the way people walk. Some individuals saunter aimlessly, moving slowly as though time is of no concern. Others will hurry, with quick, staccato steps, even if they are not in a rush. Some glide with the grace of a swan. Others move in a way that is clumsy or awkward, uncomfortable in their own skin. And on and on.

Handwriting movement reflects this same range of motion. Like body language, it reveals an individual's level of self-confidence, emotional comfort, and overall sense of well-being.

Movement is not only how handwriting happens—it's how the writer lives on the page.

Movement and Personality Structure

To review what we covered early on:

- *Space reveals the superego*—the "parent" part of personality. It reflects the writer's sense of organization, conscience, and attitudes towards authority.

- *Form reveals the ego*—the "adult" part of personality. It shows self-discipline, self-regulation, conscious controls, and how the writer presents themselves in a social context.

- *Movement reveals the id*—the "child" part of personality. It expresses the writer's core energy, instinctual drives, spontaneity, and how that energy is directed or repressed.

In general, handwriting that looks well-balanced handwriting reflects a strong ego. Rigid, overly controlled handwriting reveals a dominant superego, while wildly erratic handwriting points to an overactive id. Or, to put it more colorfully:

A balanced ego/handwriting is like a captain at the helm. When the captain grasps the wheel too tightly, the writing is stiff and inflexible. But when the id takes over and steers by impulse without a map, the writing spirals out of control.

140

Lesson Twelve
Movement and the Id

A newborn baby cannot politely request food, love, or a diaper change. It doesn't know how to wait or consider anyone else's needs. From the very beginning, the id is in charge—raw, instinctive, and single-minded. Governed by the pleasure principle, it seeks immediate gratification and avoids discomfort at all costs.

The infant's piercing cries in the middle of the night are its only means of communication, a non-negotiable demand: "Fix this now." It doesn't care that the rest of the house is asleep or that someone must get out of bed to help. At that moment, nothing matters but the urge to relieve the discomfort, whether hunger, cold, or loneliness.

For the id, the idea of waiting is foreign—it wants what it wants, and it wants it now. Only immediate satisfaction will do.

But over the first couple of years, something new begins to stir: the ego. With consistent, nurturing care, the child slowly learns to manage impulses, discovering that needs can be expressed without screaming, and that sometimes, waiting brings better results.

By around age three to five, the superego begins to take shape, like an internal voice that praises good behavior and punishes missteps. This emerging moral compass reflects the values of the child's caregivers, and later, society.

In a healthy personality, these three forces—id, ego, and superego—reach a kind of uneasy truce. The ego stands between impulse (id) and conscience (superego) mediating between the raw desires of the id and the ideals and moral guidance imposed by superego, striving to maintain balance in the self.

The handwriting of a person with a strong (healthy) ego appears well balanced (there's that phrase again!), with clear spacing and positive form. It is neither rigid nor chaotic. The sample by Carl Jung in an earlier lesson is a good example of strong ego functioning.

In contrast, poor parenting or abuse can disrupt personality development. At one extreme, a child raised by overly-strict or demanding parents—particularly in environments shaped by rigid religious doctrine—may develop an overactive superego.

This internalized voice of authority becomes a relentless inner critic, repeating unkind jibes like, "you're not good enough," "you don't measure up," "you'd better try harder." Long into adulthood, those old inner messages can continue playing in an endless loop, making one feel as though a miniature parent is sitting on their shoulder, whispering in their ear.

Handwriting that demonstrates an overdeveloped superego is rigid and overly controlled; it may even appear regimented in some cases.

To fully understand movement in handwriting, we must explore its various components. These include:

- *Zones*
- *Rhythm*
- *Ductus*
- *Pressure*
- *Speed*
- *Connectedness*
- *Trend*
- *Slant*
- *Size.*

The sample of a hyper-religious person below, with it's extremely tall, narrow upper zone, is typical of this pattern. The and imposes strict rules and expectations on his family that he may not follow himself. He functions as a stern taskmaster, guided more by internalized commands than by flexibility of emotional warmth.

My mother prayed to God, without accurate
knowledge, that she would have a male child. She
prayed to Him that if she did she would do
her best to bring him up to worship and serve
God. This is what she told me at an early

At the opposite end of the parenting spectrum are those who set few—if any—boundaries. Without structure or consistent limits, the child never learns to wait, to self-soothe, or to consider others. The id remains in the at the helm, unchecked and demanding.

My second
childhood memory
is of being dropped
off at the
nursery. I was
angry & grabbed

As the child grows, so does the expectation of self-control, but if the ground-work hasn't been laid, the ability to delay gratification never takes root. The result is an adult who, much like an infant, expects the world to respond instantly to his needs and demands immediate satisfaction without considering the consequences. When things don't go his way, he may lash out, slamming doors, shouting or sulking—emotional tantrums in grown-up form.

Such behavior is unpleasant but may be tolerable in a toddler, but in an adult, it's not just unpleasant—it can be destructive.

An "id handwriting," like the sample below, can be wild and uncontrolled, mirroring the person's impulsive behavior. The writing reflects a lack of discipline and emotional regulation. We might fairly describe this kind of behavior as childish.

The next sample is likewise impulsive but with slightly greater control. The sample above has a better spatial arrangement.

Now, let's turn to an example of a far more moderately balanced movement. There is a lot of movement in the sample below, but here, the id is tempered by the ego's guiding influence. The writing is fast, with a smooth, rhythmic flow.

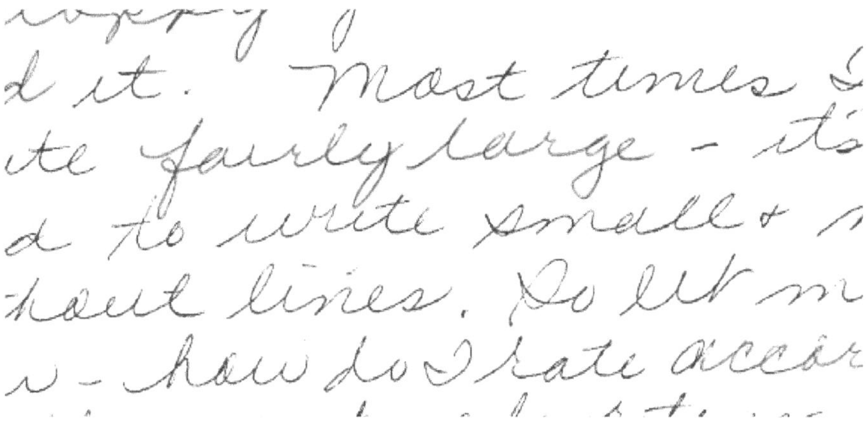
d it. Most times I
te fairly large - it's
d to write small + s
hout lines. So let m
n - how do I rate accor

This sample of diet guru **Jenny Craig** shows a strong ego.

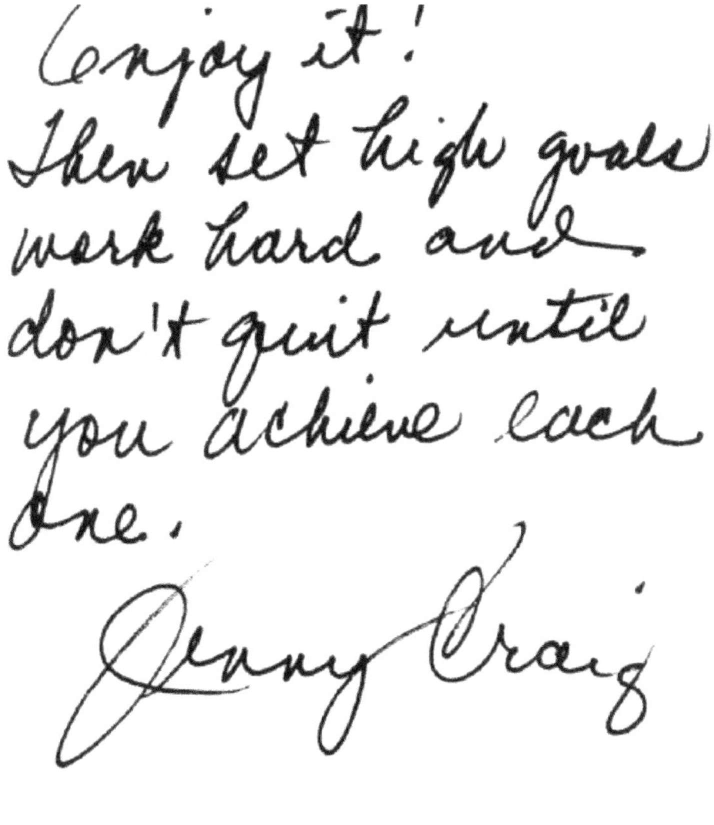
Enjoy it!
Then set high goals
work hard and
don't quit until
you achieve each
one.
Jenny Craig

Lesson Thirteen
The Movement Continuum

As Jung observed, to truly move forward, we must first look back. Handwriting—an outward expression of inward movement—offers a continuous record of psychological dialogue

On the strong-weak-disturbed continuum, strong movement in handwriting reveals itself as natural, fluid and unforced. Earlier in the course, we examined the subtle differences between form-consciousness and persona writing; the distinction between them lies not just in appearance, but in movement.

Movement is shaped mainly by rhythm and speed—two elements we'll explore in depth throughout this section. For now, know this: when movement becomes erratic or inconsistent, it signals disturbance. The greater the variation, the deeper the disruption.

There are many different types of rhythm—think of the many dance rhythms: waltz, samba, tarantella, cha cha, etc. Here are some definitions:

- *Movement or variation characterized by the regular recurrence or alternation of different quantities or conditions; e.g.: the rhythm of the tides.*

- *The patterned, recurring alternations of contrasting elements of sound or speech.*

- *Procedure or routine characterized by regularly recurring elements*

Natural movement contains the ebb and flow of rhythm—a subtle, complex quality we'll examine closely. In well-balanced handwriting, movement is not over-emphasized, it doesn't draw attention to itself; it simply supports the overall structure with quiet confidence and quietly reinforces the structure.

Strong movement in handwriting points to a writer with self-confidence and focused will. Propelled by **dynamic energy** that spurs them on and helps them pursue their goals and objectives with enthusiasm and control, the movement in their writing carries the momentum of inner conviction. They aren't

147

easily rattled by the unknown; assuming other supporting signs align, they face new challenges with a steady hand and composed determination.

The following sample, written by a middle-aged business owner, displays **strong** movement. The fast, simplified script, with a mixture of pared-down letter forms and a reasonably good spatial arrangement reflects a high level of intelligence .

Weak Movement

Weak movement sits close to the copybook school model on the continuum. Lacking strong rightward progression, it tends to sit passively on the page. Pressure is usually medium to light, and speed hovers in the medium-slow range. Leftward trend may be observed.

The more self-conscious and contrived the writing looks, the weaker the movement.

The horizontal expansion of the writing line is typically compressed—the handwriting doesn't stretch outward with vitality, but remains confined to a limited, "safe" space. In some cases, weak movement arises from excessive control, resulting in rigidity as appears.

The following sample illustrates this: Despite a right slant, the narrowness in the letter forms significantly slows the writing.

148

As briefly discussed with you on the phone yesterday, I am presently in a great deal of confusion and frustration in regards to my next job and career.

Whether the writing clings to traditional copybook standards or becomes artificially embellished and ornate, both reflect weak movement—demonstrating a lack of natural progression, positive development, and psychological growth. The writer holds fast to what they were originally taught, unable to fully evolve. In this sense, rigid "**superego**" writing fits squarely within the category of weak movement.

The following sample, although written in a copybook style, is not entirely lacking in movement. It is included here to illustrate handwriting that falls the middle of the movement continuum—neither fully strong nor entirely weak.

I am the third and youngest child in my family. As a child growing up in Freeport, Illinois, I was involved in Girl Scouts, swim club and ballet. I was raised and confirmed in our German Lutheran Church. In high school I was a cheerleader, secretary/treasurer of our class, belonged to Pep Club, German Club, and the Business Club. I graduated in the top ten percent of our class. I also felt honored to be the

149

This kind of writing shows control and conformity, yet still retains enough natural flow to avoid being classified a rigid or disturbed. Note, however, the extreme word spaces have some impact on the gestalt

More often than not, the writer of weak movement is conventional and conservative. Absent strong contradicting features, they may be inclined to wait and see what others in their social group* do before making decisions or taking action. There is typically a low degree of inner motivation, with limited energy available for pursuit of achievement or risk-taking.

---

*Note: *"Social group" may refer to peers, colleagues, or the broader cultural environment in which the writer operates, and that may not be a conventional one. "Social group" could be a gang, sports team, religious organization, etc.*

Disturbed Movement

Disturbed movement results in an especially inharmonious gestalt and is easily identified. The high degree of variability in spacing, letter size, form, direction, and other elements of writing demonstrate a lack of control over the pen and the writing movement. You may observe exaggerated upper and/or lower loops—wide and long or tall—as well as broad expansion on all planes.

This style is categorized as "id writing"—a reflection of a lack of control and impulsive, emotionally driven behavior.

The writer who produces disturbed movement tends to be excitable and spontaneous to the point of unpredictability. You can't anticipate what they'll do next. This is not a sign of a strong ego. Instead, it points to anxiety and impulsiveness, and difficulty committing to a clear course of action. The writer tends to follow immediate impulses, doing with whatever feels good at the moment, rather than making a plan, considering long-term consequences, and sticking to it.

150

In gestalt analysis, we always consider the whole picture. When a sample appears imbalanced or disturbed, look closer to determine whether the disturbance stems from space, form, or movement. A single element may be the primary source, but often, the disturbance involves interacting weaknesses across multiple dimensions. The sample below is full of extreme variability in movement that's all over the place. The has created a disturbed gestalt.

This id sample was written by the late singer, **Amy Winehouse.**

The next writing is lively and active, but has somewhat more control.

151

In the next lesson we'll take a closer look at how rhythm shapes the quality of movement and gives rise to its many variations.

Before we examine rhythm in greater detail, though, it's helpful to visualize how movement manifests across a spectrum. The chart below illustrates the continuum from from extremely controlled movement (contraction), which is rigid and inhibited, to extremely released movement, which appears chaotic or unrestrained. Most handwriting falls somewhere between these two extremes.

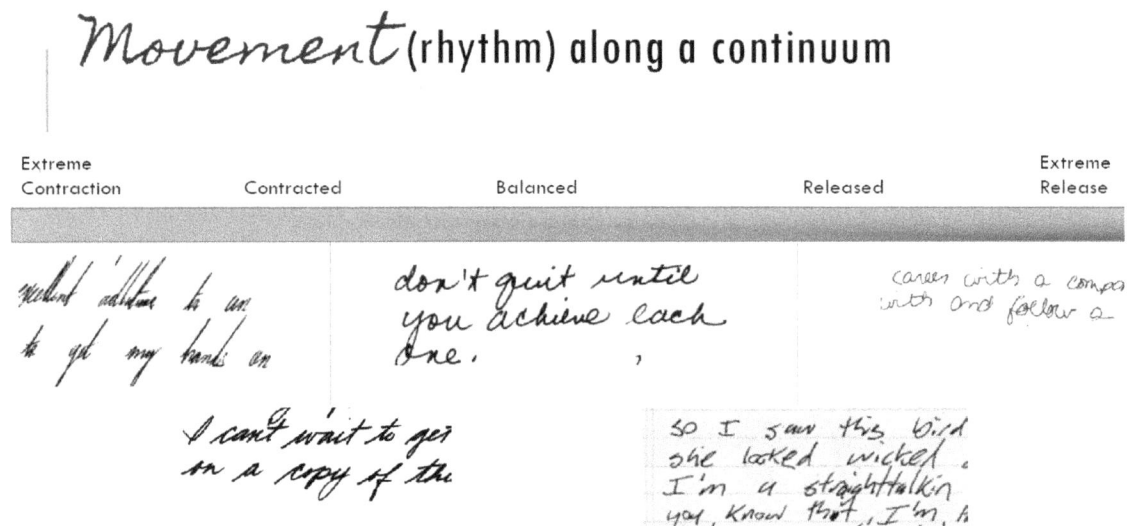

Movement (rhythm) along a continuum

Extreme Contraction	Contracted	Balanced	Released	Extreme Release

152

Lesson Fourteen
The Rhythm Continuum

Rhythm in handwriting mirrors the rhythm of life—whether in walking, speaking, or simply moving through the world. It arises through alternating patterns of contraction and release, echoing the writer's internal pulse. Like the tides that ebb and flow, handwriting moves in cycles of tension and release, moving away from the body and returning toward it. These rhythmic cycles offer a window into the writer's emotional state, energy level and capacity for self-control.

Rhythm is the heartbeat of handwriting. It underlies movement, which we have examined through the strong-weak-disturbed continuum. Now, we go deeper.

Key Principle: Look for the balance between contraction and release. Neither extreme is ideal. A healthy personality demonstrates rhythmic flexibility and resilience.

How Rhythm Manifests

- *An energetic person shows lively, **bouncing** handwriting rhythm.*

- *A gentle, soft-spoken person shows smooth, **flowing** rhythm.*

- *Someone depressed or depleted often shows **slack** rhythm, lacking energy or strength.*

153

Types of Rhythm in Handwriting

The rhythm continuum spans from extremely regular to highly irregular, each end reflecting a different psychological state and level of emotional control.

Balanced, Steady Rhythm (ego writing):

- *Reflects a strong ego and a healthy balance between control and emotional release.*
- *Indicates strong emotional regulation, inner stability, and the capacity to respond rather than react.*
- *The rhythm is natural, expressive, and human—neither mechanical nor chaotic*

Thought you might like a copy of our school catalogue as well. Dr. Pecci is the President and teaches classes as well as workshops.

Released Rhythm (Extreme Release / toward id writing):

- *Shows lack of control, impulsiveness, and poor self-discipline*
- *The writer is driven by immediate emotions and instinct, with little regard for consequences.*
- *The rhythm is chaotic, inconsistent, and emotionally charged.*
- *Suggests emotional volatility, instability, lack of internal filtering.*

If there is any change in your fee since the last time please let me know and I'll send you the balance

154

Contracted Rhythm (moderate control / towards superego writing):

- *Reflects overcontrol and, emotional suppression.*

- *The writer appears rigid, perfectionistic, and excessively self-disciplined.*

- *Emotional expression is tightly held in, often at the cost of spontaneity or authenticity.*

- *Resembles a highly regimented march—precise, constricted, and emotionally flat.*

- *Over time, emotional repression may lead to sudden explosive outbursts with severe consequences*

Understanding Regularity in Handwriting Rhythm

Rhythm is a type of routine defined by regularly recurring elements that form consistent, but not identical, patterns. In natural handwriting, rhythm shows variation within regularity, offering a glimpse into the writer's internal tempo. Patterns that are so rigid as to be nearly identical are extreme have a negative interpretation.

Key Characteristics of Regularity:

Orderly, even, or symmetrical

- *Extremely regular handwriting may resemble a computer font—mechanical and lacking the warmth and individuality of human expression.*

In conformity with fixed procedures or principle

- *Excessive regularity reflects rigid thinking and behavior. Such individuals often struggle with flexibility or change.*

155

Periodic—occurring at fixed intervals

- *A steady, repeating rhythm suggests predictability and control, contributing to the overall impression of order.*

Unvarying; constant

- *When there is little to no variation, the handwriting may feel compulsive. it suggests a controlling personality or a desire to maintain tight control over one's emotional environment.*

Formally correct or proper

- *This style reflects emotional reserve and formality. The writer may come across as constrained or overly self-conscious in social interactions.*

How to Evaluate Regularity:

To assess the degree of regularity in a handwriting sample, we observe at how consistently the writing returns to the baseline.

1.   If the writing is on unlined paper, use a ruler to draw a line beneath one of the written lines on a photocopy (do not mark the original).

2.   Examine how often all the "legs" of the letter *m* touch the ruled or imagined baseline.

3.   Check the bottoms of letters such as *o* and *a*. Do they rest squarely on the line, or do they hover above or dip below it. The more consistently the letters cling to the baseline as in the illustration below, the more regular the handwriting.

all the letters baseline

We all need to feel safe and in control of our environment, but this type of regularity reflects a particularly strong need for security and predictability. Often this need is rooted in a desire for financial or material stability—not necessarily out of materialism, but because those things represent safety and control.

Highly regular handwriting conveys the picture of a conservative, disciplined individual who prioritizes order and predictability. While this can indicate reliability and self-control, when taken to an extreme, it reveals rigidity, perfectionism, and an over-controlled personality.

As you study the following examples of regularity in handwriting, pay close attention to the uniformity in spacing and letter formation. In the first handwriting below, although the overall baseline is irregular, *each individual word adheres closely to its own internal baseline*—the downstrokes reliably return to the imaginary baseline.

This creates a subtle conflict: the **form** is regular and restrained, while the **movement** is irregular. Such tension suggests an internal struggle—this writer wants to express himself more freely, but strong needs for control restrain the impulse and hold him back.

The next sample appears rigid due to its linear, upright stance and regularity with many narrow letters. The spatial arrangement is noticeably crowded, which adds to the overall tension. Once again, we see signs of internal conflict.

The strong, consistent form, suggests a well-developed ego in someone who wants to maintain control and present herself with confidence. However, the tense, compressed movement within a crowded spatial arrangement reveals internal emotional pressure and difficulty finding ease or freedom in expression, as we saw in the previous sample, but manifested in different ways someone who is knowledgable about sports, enjoys events. Intelligence is a must, as is good sense of personality I'm looking for someone who, if I have where I have to network q "work the room" they q not have to be babysat. I'm looking for a MAN make decisions q take control of a situation. Yet

Moving along the continuum, this interesting handwriting has fairly strong regularity, but also enough rounded strokes to save it from rigidity. The leftward leaning personal pronoun I may indicate guilt of some type.

Obviously, I need to be with someone with su Compatibility is important. I need a man who is and enjoys animals. I need someone who is and who will treat my daughter like his own to be patient with my faults - help me work a and ignore others. I want to admire him an im to need me. He needs to be secure and

At the far end of the continuum is this highly released sample written by a woman in her 50s. The lack of control reflects impulsive emotions and unrestrained behavior. The writing moves erratically across the page, with inconsistent rhythm, a clear indicator of internal instability

At the same time, the double-looped ovals and frequent middle zone interference suggests that much remains hidden. This writer holds onto secrets, concealing parts of herself even as her outer expression seems inhibited.

158

The combination of uncontrolled movement and symbolic enclosure points to emotional turbulence beneath a surface of expressive release.

2. What kind of person are you interested in or looking for:

Extreme Regularity and Overcontrol

When taken to an extreme, overly regular handwriting resembles a mechanical font—precise, uniform, and devoid of natural variation. This type of over-control may be seen individuals with serious mental disturbances, including those labeled criminally insane. The handwriting conveys a sense of someone exerting tight control in an effort to contain powerful, unmanageable impulses.

We saw a striking example of this earlier in the handwriting of kidnapper-rapist Philip Garrido. Notably, over time behind bars the handwriting of many incarcerated serial offenders tends to evolve toward this excessively controlled style, as their need for internal containment intensifies.

On the control-release continuum, this writing style demonstrates a severe lack of emotional release. Emotions are tightly contained—sealed off until, like a pressure cooker without a vent, they eventually explode with disproportionate or destructive consequences.

Why This Happens

Institutional settings such as prisons impose strict external control. Inmates are required to follow rigid routines and comply with a tightly regulated environment, which suppresses their ability to act on violent or impulsive urges.

159

Yet, the underlying emotional and psychological drives that fuel those urges do not simply vanish. Instead, they remain active beneath the surface, building in intensity.

In such environments, handwriting can become a silent outlet—a form of expression that reveals the internal pressure simmering beneath the enforced calm exterior. What cannot be spoken or acted upon may surface in the writing, offering critical insight into the writer's unspoken emotional state.

Case Example: Aileen Wuornos

The handwriting of female serial killer Aileen Wuornos—whose life was dramatized in the 2003 film, *Monster*—is a marked example of over-control. Her writing is rigid, highly controlled, and lacking in natural variation—hallmarks of emotional suppression.

Imagine the level of muscular and psychological control required to maintain the kind of regularity seen in Wuornos' script. While it may appear neat and precise at first glance, the mechanical quality of the writing betrays the truth: this is not order for clarity's sake, but a reflection of extreme inner restraint. The form becomes a mask—one that hides volatile emotions seething beneath the surface. In addition, note the odd, inexplicable slashes that appear above the *Js* in *Jew*.

From what we have thus far learned of the Antichrist, the probability is that he will be a Syrian Jew, for it is not likely that the Jews will accept as their Messiah one who is not a Jew, unless the claimant by false pretense makes them believe he is one. This however, does not prevent the Antichrist being a **Roman Citizen** and the political head of the revived Roman Empire, for Saul of Tarsus was both a Jew and a Roman Citizen.

Serial Murderer Aileen Wuornos, executed in 2002

Irregularity in Handwriting

At the opposite end of the regularity spectrum lies highly irregular hand-writing that results from disturbances across all areas of the gestalt—what we refer to as *id writing*. While the writer with highly regular handwriting seeks to suppress or contain emotion, to always be in control, the highly irregular writer expresses emotional freely, often excessively.

Highly irregular writers:

- *Lack consistency in thought and action*
- *Struggle with commitment, frequently reversing decisions*
- *Act impulsively, driven by mood rather than logic*
- *Display emotional instability, shifting quickly from one state to another*

This unfiltered emotional expression can make the person appear sponta-neous and creative—but also erratic unreliable and difficult to rely on.

Example: Elvis Presley

A good example of irregularity can be seen in the handwriting of Elvis Pres-ley in an excerpt from a letter he wrote to President Richard Nixon in 1970, offering his services as a narc.

Elvis Presley, King of Rock and Roll

161

The handwriting displays extreme inconsistency. Notice the frequent changes in letter size, slant, and form—sometimes dramatic changes within a single line. There is no unifying rhythm or structural coherence, which mirrors the writer's internal instability. The original was written in red ink.

Elvis wanted to help in the fight against drugs and communism. His multipage letter became a highly requested image from the National Archives, and can be obtained by searching Google Images. President Nixon met with Elvis in the Oval Office and gave him a federal narcotics badge.

Seven years later, Elvis died at the age of 42. The official cause of death was a heart attack, ironically, with drug use as a contributing factor. Whether substance abuse affected the handwriting sample above is unknown, but would not be surprising.

Lesson Fifteen
The Three Zones

In both major methods of handwriting analysis, handwriting is symbolically divided into three zones—**upper, middle,** and **lower**—each reflecting a different aspect of the writer's personality. Just as a building has different levels with distinct purposes, handwriting expresses multiple layers of psychological function. While it is important to understand what each zone symbolizes individually, they are always part of an interconnected whole. The zones work together dynamically to reveal the deeper structure of personality and its meaning within handwriting.

---

*As a helpful visual anchor, note that in cursive copybooks only one lowercase letter—the **letter** f—extends through all three zones.*

Energy and the Zones

Just as water can transform into ice, steam, or liquid depending on circumstances, our basic life force—our psychological energy—can also manifest in different forms. Handwriting reveals how that energy is distributed among the three zones, depending on what is needed at the moment.

The following breakdown shows how each zone reflects a different domain of personality. Note, too, that energy shifts continuously between the zones, responding to the demands of the moment. In a healthy personality, the energy flows in a dynamic interplay between the zones, adjusting to the writer's psychological and situational needs as they change.

163

Upper Zone — abstract thought, ideals, imagination, conscience, spirituality

Middle Zone — social interaction, daily life, self-image

Lower Zone — physicality, instincts, material, and sensual needs

Zonal Imbalance and Over-emphasis

Sometimes a writer places too much energy into one or two zones at the expense of the others. This over-emphasis can take different forms:

- *Disproportionate height or width of letters in a particular zone*

- *Exaggerated loops or over-elaboration of form or letter design*

- *Unnecessary initial or final strokes that move inappropriately into the upper or lower zone*

Such imbalance tells us where the writer channels their energy—and often, their psychological preoccupations. For example, In **Elvis Presley's** handwriting, which we looked at in the previous lesson, the **lower zone** is disproportionately long (and sometimes extremely wide). This suggests a powerful focus on physical needs and material pursuits such as food, sex, money, physical activity.

The Middle Zone: Where We Live

The **middle zone** (MZ) of handwriting contains the body of lowercase letters that rest on or connect at the baseline. It reflects everyday social functioning, communication, and self-image. The middle zone includes:

- *Lowercase vowels: a, e, i, o, u*
- *Consonants: c, j, m, n, r, s, t, v, w, x*
- *Middle parts of letters that also enter other zones, such as:*
  - *The circle of the letter b and d*
  - *The buckle of h and k*
  - *The circle part of g, p, and q*
  - *The "bucket" of y and the upper curve of z*
  - *The middle part of f*

164

The baseline serves as the dividing line between reality and the subconscious. Sitting at the bottom of the middle zone, it defines the boundary between the middle and the lower zone.

Symbolic Meanings of the Middle Zone

The middle zone represents how one interacts with the immediate environment—the world of real people and practical activities. Considered by graphologists to be the most important zone, as that is the area of reality, where day-to-day life happens, and the writer expresses:

- *Self-image (ego needs and ego strength)*
- *Everyday social functioning*
- *Attitudes toward oneself and others*

Felix Klein described the lower zone as the "basement" of the psyche, where memories, instincts, and unconscious drives are stored.

Upper and Lower Zones in Context

As described above, the lower zone begins at the baseline and includes descenders like: g, j, p, y, z,f, as well as letter parts that inappropriately begin or fall below it—a cue to examine energetic or psychological imbalance.

Upper zone letters rise from the baseline and move away from the body, expanding up and outward, normally turning left, forming a downstroke that loops toward the body and the self. Writers who simplify their writing and do not make a loop avoid the upper zone. **Block printers**, too, focus on *downstrokes*, avoiding the upper *and* lower zones.

- *The upper zone includes:*
  - *Ascenders such as l, b, h, k, f*
  - *Capital letters*
  - *Diacritical marks, including i-dots and t-bars*

165

Taking the downstroke back to the middle zone is a way of bringing one's ideas and principles into reality so as to carry them out. An over-emphasis on the upper zone signifies a writer who expends a lot of energy on thinking and planning, but not so much on doing. Thus, the writer who finds reasons to stay in the upper zone, either by creating extra width, extra height or other elaborations, may have difficulty integrating their ideas with the *reality* of the middle zone.

Symbolism of the Upper Zone

The upper zone is a distinct area of psychological functioning which corresponds to the father archetype, superego, and the internalized social ideal. It represents the area where the present (mz) engages with the future—where possibilities are imagined, and conscience is activated. To review, it is the area of:

- *Mental activities, concrete imagination (not fantasy, which is in the lower zone)*
- *Conscience, philosophies, principles*
- *Conscious aspects of the personality*

The Lower Zone

In copybook handwriting, the lower zone begins at the baseline and extends downward below it, symbolically moving into the subconscious. The classic lower zone stroke follows this pattern:

- *A downstroke, which moves toward the writer's body*
- *It then curves to the left and reverses direction, forming an upstroke.*
- *The upstroke creates a loop and completes by moving away from the writer's body and returning to the baseline—the symbolic line of reality.*

This movement between the inner self and the outside world reflects the cyclical nature of instinct, desire, and action. As you write, notice how your hand moves toward the body in the downstroke and away from the body on the upstroke. This physical motion mirrors psychological processes—particularly in the upper zone, where writing literally reaches upward and outward, symbolizing projection beyond the self.

166

Symbolism of the Lower Zone

The lower zone casts light on the darker, unconscious side of the personality. Felix Klein compared it to digging underground, where the roots of life lie hidden. This zone contains everything that remains outside conscious awareness, including primal urges, sexual energy, material interests, the past, and the domain of the id. It is the place where deep-seated motivations and unresolved tensions reside, exerting influence from beneath the surface. To review, the lower zone represents:

- *Physical drives: food, sex, material needs*

- *Instinctual behavior, sleep patterns*

- *The unconscious or hidden aspects of the personality*

If the baseline represents the solid ground you stand one, the lower zone is the deep well from which personal energy and drive originate.

Variations in Lower Zone Formations

The copybook form may be modified in many ways:

- ***No loops***: *a straight downstroke or one that curves to the left, indicating:*
  - *restriction, inhibition, or suppressed instinct (unless only at the end of words, which may just be a simplification).*

- ***Exaggerated loops***: *extremely long and/or wide loops can indicate:*
  - *An over-investment in material or sensual concerns*
  - *A struggle to translate ideas into reality*
  - *Emotional entanglement with past experiences or unresolved needs*
- ***Staying too long*** *in the LZ, exaggerating length, width, or complexity may highlight difficulty in:*
  - *Staying grounded*
  - *Balancing the practical with the instinctual*
  - *Integrating unconscious drives with conscious action (i.e., putting dreams and ideas into practice)*

The following chart summarizes what the copybook middle zone size can mean

Middle Zone Size	Interpretation
Copybook (3 mm)	Hesitant but can grow through success; one failure may shut down future attempts.
Large (4-5 mm)	Confident, attention-seeking, enjoys the spotlight. May lack focus and require stimulation to stay engaged.
Very Large (>5 mm)	Indicates *grandiosity*, not genuine extroversion. May mask low self-worth with an inflated sense of self. Resists input.
Very Small (>2 mm)	Suggests a fragile self-concept, possible depressive. Prefers solitude and retreats into inner life. May neglect real-world responsibilities and feel overwhelmed by minor challenges.

Lesson Sixteen
Measuring the Zones

In gestalt graphology, absolute measurements are less important than developing your visual perception—what we call "eye training." Still, learning to measure the zones is a key step in building a reliable frame of reference. By understanding what qualifies as "large," "small," or "medium," you create a solid foundation for evaluating handwriting.

Once you're skilled at perceiving the overall gestalt, you won't need exact measurements—unless you want to confirm a hunch or explain your observations more precisely.

Copybook Measurements

We use copybook for our basic measurements, beginning with the middle zone, which reflects ego needs and self-concept. Most American copybooks define middle zone letters this way:

- **Height**: 3 mm

- **Width**: 3 mm

As we discussed in the previous lesson, these standards most easily apply to letters such as o and a, which the copybook form is nearly circular. Letters that exceed these dimensions are considered large; those that fall below are small.

Note: Size exists on a continuum. There are no rigid cutoffs, only relative impressions.

169

How to Measure the Zones

Use the illustration below as your reference:

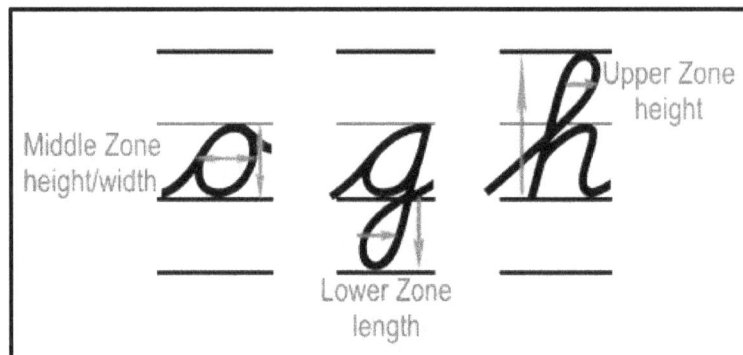

- *Middle Zone Height (MZH) — from baseline to top of MZ letters*
- *Upper Zone Height (UZH) — from baseline to top of UZ letters*
- *Lower Zone Length (LZL) — from the baseline downward to bottom of LZ letters*
- *From side-to-side (MZW/UZW/LZW) — side-to-side measurement of ovals or loops*

Understanding Zonal Proportions in Handwriting

When judging size in handwriting, it's not enough to say a letter is "big" or "small." What matters more is how the zones relate to each other proportionally. Copybook ratios that apply:

- **Middle Zone Height** (MZH) and Upper Zone Height (UZH)
- Middle Zone Height (MZH) and Lower Zone Length (LZL)

Standard copybook ratios

- MZH : UZH = 1 : 1.5
- MZH : LZH = 1 : 2.

This means, in Copybook:

- The upper zone is 1.5 times the middle zone height.
- The lower zone is 2 times as long as the middle zone height.

170

How to Calculate Proportions

1. Measure each zone in millimeters
2. Divide the longer number by the shorter

Example 1:

MZH = 3 mm, UZH = 4.5 mm

$\rightarrow 4.5 \div 3 = 1.5 \rightarrow$ ratio is 1:1.5 $\rightarrow$ Average upper zone.

Example 2:

MZH = 3 mm, UZH = 6 mm:

$\rightarrow 6 \div 3 = w \rightarrow$ Ratio is 1:2 $\rightarrow$ Expanded upper zone

What Do the Ratios Reveal?

If like me you're not fond of math, just remember:

Zonal imbalance = energy imbalance.

Such writers over-invest in certain zones to compensate for what's lacking elsewhere.

Example:

- *Small MZ*
- *Very tall UZ*
- *Short LZ*

Assuming the overall gestalt supports it, the writer is channeling most of their energy into abstract or intellectual (UZ) pursuits, neglecting daily needs (MZ) and physical grounding (LZ).

Zonal Compensation and Psychological Meaning

When one or two zones dominate, it points to compensatory behavior. The writer is trying to make up for a deficit, real or perceived, in another area.

In the above example, a very tall upper zone may indicate:

- *An authoritarian father or demanding male authority figure.*
- *Lifelong striving to meet unattainable expectations*
- *A sense of never quite being "good enough."*

171

Interpretation always depends on:
1. The overall gestalt of the handwriting
2. Which zones are over- or underdeveloped

Middle Zone Size: Ego Needs and Ego Strength

The middle zone demonstrates how we manage everyday life and social functioning. By observing the height and width of this zone, we can gain valuable insights into the writer's self-image.

Middle Zone Height (MZH): Ego Needs

The writer whose middle zone height is close to the 3mm copybook standard generally has a reasonably healthy self-image. Even if they are not fully confident, they at least recognize that they deserve to take up space in the world. A smaller MZH may reflect self-effacement or perhaps low self-worth.

Middle Zone Width (MZW): Ego Strength

Recognizing a need is not the same as feeling confident to act on it. The critical question is: does the writer feel strong enough to go out and claim what they believe is rightfully theirs? A middle zone that is slightly narrower than its height is common, but the narrower the oval letters (like *a* and *o*), the weaker the ego strength. A compressed width suggests anxiety or lack of assertiveness

Common Middle Zone Patterns and Their Implications

Copybook Size (Medium Height, Medium Width): Indicates a generally conventional personality. The writer likely has a reasonable amount of self-esteem. They may be a little hesitant to try new things and meet new people, but can do so as with some preparation and encouragement.

With some middle zone narrowness, if he is successful in an endeavor, he will probably attempt it again. On the other hand, if he feels that he did poorly and embarrasses himself, he is likely to refrain from ever repeating the experience, shrinking back even further (narrowness).

Narrow Middle Zone: points to anxiety, a reluctance to engage socially, and lacks enough *right trend*—the movement toward the future and others. The narrower the letters, the greater the anxiety and the more the person pulls away from new experiences or people.

Wide Variation in MZ Size: if the middle zone shows inconsistent height and/or width, the form is disturbed—a sign of emotional conflict and instability in self-concept. This person is apt to be moody and unreliable, shifting behavior depending on the situation or the company.

Behavioral Implications of Middle Zone Size

The size of the middle zone is a key indicator of how the writer sees themselves in the world—how much space they believe they deserve to take up, and how they express their social identity and emotional energy.

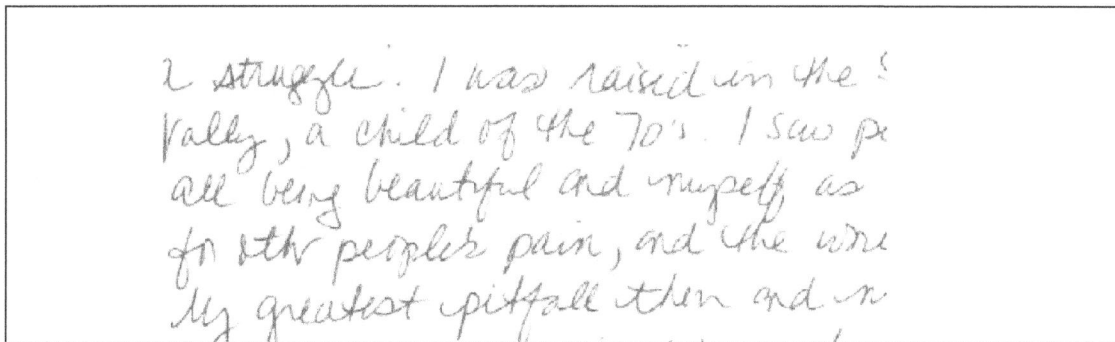

Medium overall size

Middle Zone Size and the Self-Concept

Large Middle Zone (Approximately 4-5 mm)

A writer with a large—but not extreme—middle zone typically:

- *Exudes confidence.*
- *Enjoys being noticed and loves to be in the spotlight. I*
- *Is expressive, attention-seeking, and eager to win approval, which reinforces their sense of self-worth.*

However, the large writer has a short attention span. Easily distracted and quickly bored, they require stimulation and novelty to stay engaged. Tasks or relationships that don't hold their interest may soon be abandoned as they move on to the next exciting thing.

173

Large overall size

Extremely Large Middle Zone (Greater than 5mm)

When the middle zone exceeds 5 mm in height, it points to grandiosity and an inflated self-focus. This writer may:

- *Refuse to listen to others' input*
- *Believe they are always right.*
- *See themselves as central to everything.*

Despite this outward confidence, such a person is likely to be insecure or shy, and is overcompensating for low self-worth. This is not true ego strength—it's defensive self-aggrandizement.

Extremely Large

174

The sample above is a teenage girl who has no sense of "other." As far as she is concerned, the world revolves around her needs. She has no conscience (upper zone), and lives in the moment (all middle zone)/

Very Small Middle Zone (Less than 2 mm)

At the opposite end of the scale, a very small middle zone suggests a poorly developed self-concept. These writers may:

- *Appear outgoing, yet inwardly wants to disappear.*
- *Feel overwhelmed by life's demands*
- *Retreat into their inner world rather than engage socially*

Very Small Middle Zone

Though not necessarily unfriendly, they are highly introspective, often preferring solitude over external stimulation. They look inward for answers and are typically uninterested in others' opinions.

Depression is frequently a factor. Even minor obstacles seem insurmountable to this person, and without compensating strengths elsewhere in the writing, this person may withdraw entirely or give up easily.

175

The Upper Zone: Ideals, Intellect, and Authority

In copybook writing the upper zone is 4.5 mm in height—1.5 times the height of the middle zone, and 1.5mm wide, or half the width of the middle zone. Writers who follow these proportions tend to be open-minded and willing to consider new ideas, but they apply discrimination and judgment before adopting them. there is a healthy curiosity about abstract or future-oriented concepts, but with boundaries.

Tall and Wide Upper Zone

An exaggeratedly tall and wide upper zone is associated with excessive idealism or unrealistic thinking, and has been observed in:

- *Highly religious individuals, especially males in positions of authority.*
- *Unreliable individuals who may not follow through on commitments.*
- *Sexual offenders in prison populations, particularly rapists and other abusers (a correlation noted in multiple case studies, though not exclusive to them).*

This zone expresses a surge of energy toward ideals, fantasies, and abstract thinking, often coupled with emotionalism and a lack of groundedness. When the loops are too large, the writer may:

- *Be emotionally reactive and hypersensitive.*
- *Take things personally, even when unintended.*
- *Be prone to imaginative excess or escapism.*

As always, you must interpret this feature within the context of the writing. In the writing below, the gestalt is negative due to the sharp, pointed strokes and double-crossed t-s, which disturb the form.

176

Tall and Narrow Upper Zone

When the upper zone is very tall but narrow, it often signals:

- *Rigid thinking and rejection of new ideas*
- *A "do as I say, not as I do" mentality. '*
- *Likely upbringing in authoritarian or highly religious households, often involving a dominant or potentially abusive father figure or substitute authority (e.g., stepfather, older brother, uncle, teacher, minister).*

Writers with this style tend to:

- *Enforce rules but may not follow them personally*
- *Seek authority roles, such as military, law enforcement, or hierarchical institutions.*
- *Exhibit limited empathy for different viewpoints.*

Example: The young male sales professional below exhibits extremely tall and narrow upper zones—an unexpected career alignment but one which may reflect a persuasive style backed by internal rigidity.

Wide Upper Zone (Moderate Height)

A moderately tall, wide upper zone reflects:

- *Creative imagination and openness to new ideas.*
- *Tendency to explore possibilities and consider alternatives.*
- *Potential for emotional sensitivity and vulnerability if the loops are too exaggerated.*

These individuals may be idealistic and optimistic, though occasionally un-tethered from practicality. The following writing, however, hugs the printed baseline and has strong regularity, so there may be a better balance.

Very Short Upper Zone

When the upper zone is barely present, the writer is typically:

- *Pragmatic and grounded in the here-and-now.*
- *Disinterested in theory, philosophy, or long-range planning.*
- *Self-reliant and skeptical of external authority—be it a boss, parent, or even a deity.*

Often found in women, this style may indicate:

- *Lack of paternal influence—either absent or ineffective fathers.*
- *Preference for concrete goals and visible, measurable results.*
- *Best performance when given clear expectations and accountability.*

Example: Next, a 27-year-old woman with a minimal upper zone also showed short, narrow lower loops—underscoring a lack of abstract vision and limited interest in emotional or material expansion.

[handwritten sample]

The Lower Zone: Depths of the Psyche

The copybook lower zone is twice as long as the height of the middle zone—about 4.5 mm in length and 1.5 to 2.0 mm in width. In symbolic terms, this zone represents the unconscious, instinctual drives, and is linked with physical needs, sexuality, material concerns, and the past. The downstroke pulls toward the body (a self-protective gesture), while the upstroke moves away (a release of energy).

Compressed or Closed Lower Loops

- *Tightly closed or squeezed lower loops indicate repression instinctual drives—especially sexual or emotional ones.*

- *The energy of the id is constrained, leading to frustration, tension, or withdrawal.*

- *May appear emotionally flat or overly controlled, despite deep internal urges.*

[handwritten sample]

179

Wide Lower Loops

Moderately wide and well-formed loops allows room for fantasy, passion, and creative imagining. But excessively wide lower loops may reflect a dreamer lost in fantasy and disconnected from action:

- Tends to talk more than do.
- May express elaborate fantasies, especially sexual ones, without follow-through.
- Prone to emotional indulgence or escapism.

Incomplete Lower Zone

An incomplete loop—where the stroke does not return to the baseline—signals unresolved emotional issues, particularly from the past.

Two forms of incompletion:

1. **Abrupt stop** (straight downstroke, no return):

   - Writer begins to access emotional material but withdraws due to comfort.
   - Reflects a refusal to examine or process painful past experiences.

180

The previous writing is an extreme example of a straight downstroke.

When the straight, unlooped lower zone is at the end of a word it is a simplification and has less weight than when it appears mid-word.

---

2. **Cradle-shaped or garland stroke** (open to the left):

   ○ *A regression to an unmet need for nurturing.*

   ○ *The writer unconsciously seeks mothering or protection, often in inappropriate places.*

When parts of letters that should be in the middle zone, such as *h* or *n*, dip into the lower zone inappropriately, it shows searching for emotional fulfillment in areas where it cannot be found.

The next writing is a middle-aged male. The one below that is a female in her thirties.

Unusual Variations in the Lower Zone

- **Snail-shell** *(concentric inward spirals):*

  - *Highly self-protective and self-involved.*

  - *Reflects deep retreat into the self; difficulty opening up emotionally.*

> *that I wasn't ready to get married... that maybe the lack*
> *sign.... I know that this isn't something you usually disc*
> *going to be honest + tell the whole story, I have to – I*
> *that sex just wasn't the way it used to be...... and we*
> *and all these things started scaring me. I talked ab*
> *all said that it was just pre-wedding jitters or cold fee*

- **Capping off** *(crossing the downstroke before reaching the baseline):*

  - *Indicates a specific unresolved emotional trauma.*

  As described by Dr. Christian Dettweiler:

  - *The graphologist can guesstimate the approximate age at which the trauma occurred:*
  - *The downstroke represents a timeline from birth (bottom) to the present (baseline).*
  - *If the upstroke crosses the downstroke mid-way, for example, trauma likely occurred at that point in the writer's life.*

> *my love a very happy woman.*
> *I am in the process of developing a*
> *shopping center in Moorpark. Over the years I*
> *done a little work in real estate too. I was*
> *pleased to see that your return address is is*
> *. . . . . Hills. so that ma*

182

Example: if the writer was 40 years old at the time of writing, and the upstroke crossed the downstroke at about ¼ of the way up, the trauma would have occurred around age 10. If there are several different points at which the upstroke crosses, it signifies multiple unresolved traumas at various ages.

Variable Lower Zone

When the lower zone is inconsistent in size, shape, or width, it reveals emotional insecurity and lack of inner cohesion.

The writer may:

- *Start strong but lose interest of motivation quickly.*
- *Be easily discouraged and seek constant external validation.*
- *Experience fluctuating confidence and commitment.*

Twists and Turns in the Lower Zone

Symbolic of the Unconscious and the Instinctual Self

In Gestalt handwriting analysis, the lower zone represents the id—the instinctual and libidinal energy of the personality. When this energy is misdirected or disturbed, the loops in the lower zone may take on twisted, angular, or otherwise distorted forms—and there are many, many variations—each carrying its only psychological message. Just a few are provided here.

Twisted Lower Loops

When the lower zone shows twisted or entangled loops it reflects a misdirection of sexual or libidinal energy. In most cases, such forms are associated with a history of childhood sexual trauma. The individual's sense of self and sexual identity has been profoundly altered, often leading to:

- *Deep shame and internal conflict*
- *Sexual repression or compulsivity*
- *Emotional dysregulation*

While both men and women may exhibit this feature, it is more often observed in women's handwriting. In this case there are twisted and angular forms.

183

[handwritten note: "I can't thank you enough for the wonderful day with you. You are such a good friend and so generous with your time! Let's discuss your New York ... no ready."]

The Felon's Claw

A particular variation known as a the "felon's claw" consists of arcade-formed lower loops that resemble claw-like structures. Despite its unfortunate name, this form is:

- *More frequently seen in women with a history of sexual abuse than actual felons.*

- *Found in any zone, but particularly meaningful in the lower zone, where it is associated with:*

- *Guilt tied to a sexual experience.*

- *A persistent need to revisit past trauma, especially sexual abuse.*

- *A tendency to form relationships with abusive partners, unconsciously attempting to "rewrite" the original trauma—a pattern that typically leads to re-traumatization rather than healing.*

- *Identifies a need to cover up sexual trauma that left the writer feeling guilty and ashamed, despite being the victim.*

[handwritten note: "someone intelligent and well-educated, with a wide range of interests and, of course, a great sense of humor. Someone thoughtful, kind and emotionally secure. But, also, someone who is open-minded and creative. Someone with depth."]

Tied and Knotted Lower Loops

When the lower loops are tied up in knots, it signifies extreme repression or distortion of id energy. For example:

Case Study: A woman raised by strict missionary parents in the early 20th century later engaged in an incestuous relationship with sons. Her handwriting in her late 60s, shown next, displays:

- *Knotted lower loops*
- *A rigid, authoritarian quality—indicative of a dominant superego*
- *In addition, frequent bouts of asthma were potentially related to unconscious guilt and a need to maintain control*
- *A form of emotional blackmail: family members were conditioned to believe that upsetting her could result in a medical crisis.*

These tightly knotted lower loops show the libidinal energy twisting back on itself, unable to move freely toward satisfaction, resulting in distorted behavior and deep internal conflict.

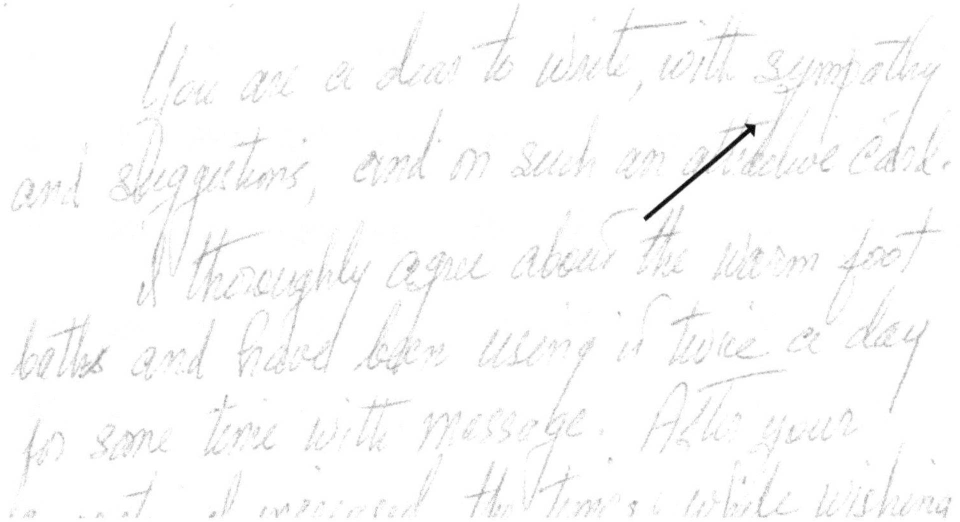

Separation of Middle and Lower Zones

Sometimes, the middle zone part (circle) of a letter is detached from its lower loop. This reflects a complete psychological split between the writer's day-to-day functioning (ego) and sexual identity (id).

Example: The son of the woman mentioned above shows this detachment, symbolizing the psychological impact of the incest. His life history—marked by

185

addiction, psychiatric hospitalization, and attempted suicide—mirrors the all-but unresolvable inner conflict his handwriting reveals, shown below.

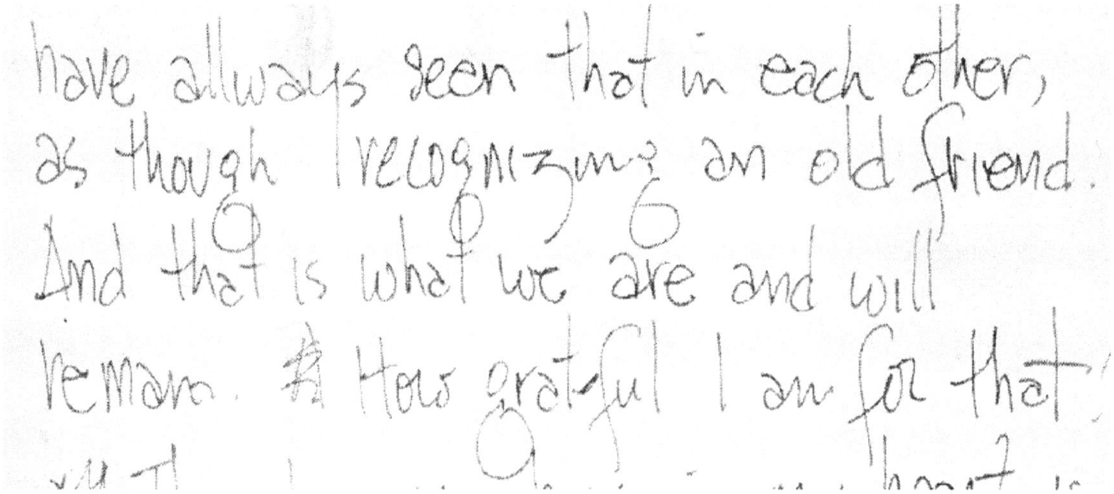

This sample of a woman in her 20s also displays the g split in two.

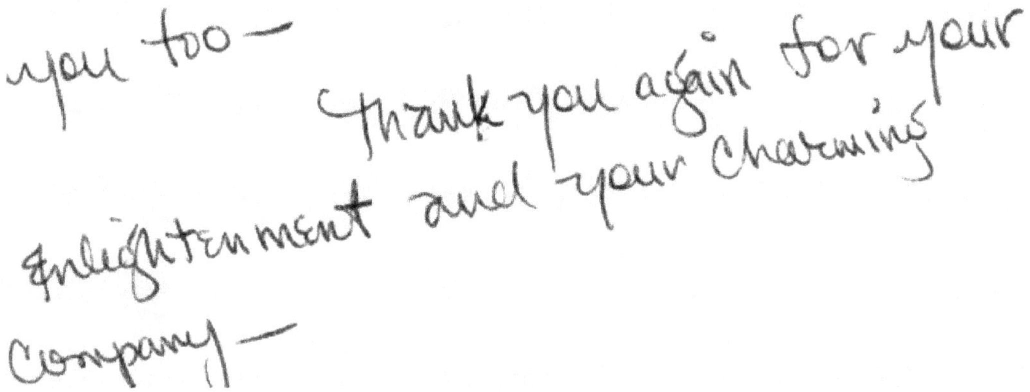

Leftward-pulled loops (less common):

- *Indicate a longing for maternal comfort or care.*
- *Often found in men with absent or threatening fathers.*
- *The mother-child bond is strong, but may not be emotionally healthy.*

186

[handwriting sample]

Rightward-pulled loops:

- *Indicate resistance toward male authority.*
- *Attachment to mother*

In the next sample, note that not only do the lower loops pull to the right, the *h* moves inappropriately into the lower zone. Suggesting the writer harbors resentment or rebellion against a father figure or dominant male influences.

[handwriting sample]

Here is another example of right-pulling lower loops in a very different gestalt. How do you interpret it?

[handwriting sample]

187

Angles in the Lower Zone

Angles where they should be rounded loops reflect hostility—especially when they appear in the lower zone. Since this zone symbolizes the hidden or unconscious, the aggression may not be overtly expressed, but remain deeply seated. In this sample, however, the gestalt suggests that the aggression comes into the middle zone and may be acted upon.

Sharpness of the angles determines intensity:

In former President Bill Clinton's handwriting, the angles are softened and co-exist with rounded forms, suggesting tempered aggression rather than overt hostility.

Final Note on Zones

As always in Gestalt analysis, no single indicator stands alone. Lower zone formations must be evaluated in the context of the entire handwriting sample—taking into account spacing, movement, form, and other elements to understand how the id interacts with the ego and superego.

There are many more possibilities than can be discussed here. In my book, *Advanced Studies in Handwriting Psychology*, there is a chapter dedicated to the lower zone and the subconscious.

Lesson Seventeen
The Connectedness Continuum

Connectedness refers to the quality and degree to which letters are joined together in handwriting. Like all other elements of graphic expression, this feature carries meaning on multiple levels of personality functioning. The degree of connection reflects both cognitive processes and emotional or social needs and tendencies.

A related word—*ligature*—is borrowed from forensic science, where it refers to the material used to tie or strangle a victim. In handwriting analysis, however, the meaning is benign—it simply refers to the connecting stroke that links letters together.

To connect means

- *To become joined, united.*
- *Letters linked in a uniform, continuous flow (copybook model).*
- *To establish a rapport or relationship; relate.*
- *Any relationship between things*
- *The process of bringing together ideas or events in memory or imagination*
- *Connectedness reveals the writer's ability to synthesize information, recall events, and conceptualize theoretical constructs.*

In handwriting, the degree of connectedness—how many letters are bound together—gives insight into how easily the writer relates to others and establishes rapport.

Can there be too much connectedness?

Copybook instruction teaches students to connect all the letters in a word. Moreover, some copybook models also promote other negative habits that graphologists recommend discarding—such as elaborate capitals. Connected-

191

ness is no exception. Some breaks in connection are both natural and desirable. For example, breaking connections after syllables is acceptable and often reflects natural rhythm. But breaks in unexpected places—such as after the first letter, or just before the last letter—are less appropriate and may signal processing difficulties or interruptions in thought.

Many abrupt breaks can reflect issues in personality functioning.

On one end of the continuum, some writers closely follow copybook and connect all of their letters, including capitals. At the opposite extreme is highly disconnected writing, with many gradations in between.

A writer who connects all letters—including capitals—is said to be over-connecting. This reflects a pragmatic, down-to-earth, realistic individual with few illusions, like the writer whose handwriting appears next, a successful real estate broker in his sixties who had a reputation for being argumentative.

Such a writer tends to string ideas together in a logical sequence and may be impatient with interruptions that disrupt the flow of thought. Especially when accompanied by medium to heavy pressure, this pattern indicates a good memory for facts and details.

Depending on the gestalt, highly connected writing can point to a logical, linear thinker—or to someone who is rigid, argumentative, and unwilling to let go of the argument until the other person gives in.

Highly connected writers often exhibit strong needs for interaction and difficulty letting go of people, ideas, or situations, even when it would be healthier to do so. The degree of connectedness—how many letters connect in a group—must, as always, be evaluated in the context of the whole writing.

Just as hugging the baseline reveals a need for security and symbolically keeps the writer's "feet firmly on the ground," highly connected writing by its nature tends to stay close to the baseline. When this is not the case—i.e., when highly connected script exhibits a highly variable baseline—this contradiction reveals strong underlying conflict. These two characteristics do not naturally coexist and warrant deeper exploration.

Disconnected writing

In this section, we focus on disconnected cursive writing. Printing represents a different form of disconnection and was covered in Lesson Ten.

When analyzing disconnected cursive, observe the breaks between letters to determine whether they are **smooth airstrokes** or **choppy and abrupt** separations.

How to distinguish the difference

- *Airstrokes occur when the pen is briefly lifted from the paper, but the writer continues its movement in the air, resuming contact with the paper in the same directional flow. These strokes show feathered endings and beginnings—thinner at the point where the pen leaves the end of one letter and returns to the page at the beginning of the next.*

- *Choppy breaks stop abruptly and involve a backward movement rather than a forward flow. There is no feathering, instead, both the ending and the beginning strokes are blunt. A magnifying lens may be necessary to distinguish these subtle differences.*

The next sample is an intellectually bright middle-aged woman who could be quite abrupt socially, like the abrupt breaks in her handwriting.

193

> I am sending you my
> preliminary efforts at
> developing questions. Before
> I continue, please tell me if
> I'm on the right track or
> not. I do need some guidance
> as to how I should proceed.

Personality indications

Writers who makes smooth breaks between letters are generally imaginative and intuitive. The gaps between the letters create a kind of open channel, allowing spontaneous bursts of intuition to enter from the upper or lower zones and find practical application in the middle zone, where it can be put to use.

The sample below is a writer in his 50s whose many breaks are mixed between smooth and abrupt.

> hum, two corrections in the
> first two words I write, inter-
> esting – well since I can
> write about anything I'll write
> about my feelings about going
> to Bouchercon. Stark terror –
> I'm an introvert, too, and the

194

Writers with abrupt or choppy breaks—blunt endings and beginnings like the one above—may generate many ideas but struggle to fully develop them. There is a tendency to jump to conclusions without the benefit of logical analysis. As a result, they may arrive at correct conclusions—but for the wrong reasons—and are prone to faulty judgment. The more uneven and choppy the breaks, the greater the writer's difficulty in maintaining emotional balance. Consistency—or lack thereof—in these breaks provides valuable insight into the writer's emotional regulation.

Here is a sample with smooth breaks

Thought processes and social behavior

The disconnected writer may be intelligent and quick-minded, but their thoughts jump and can be disjointed, making it difficult to organize ideas into coherent, a logical sequences. In addition to cognitive fragmentation, highly disconnected writers tend to experience social challenges. Their erratic thought processes can result in socially awkward or inappropriate behavior that makes others uncomfortable.

For example, consider a sample written by a law professor in his forties, who also served as editor of a legal magazine. Highly disconnected, the small size of the writing combined with broad spatial layout reflects someone whose energy is primarily channeled toward intellectual pursuits rather than social ones. Socially, this writer is shy and far more at ease in the company of one or two familiar people than in larger groups.

Soldering/Patching

Occasionally, a writer will break a connection between letters, then place the next stroke directly on top of the previous one, creating the appearance that the letters are connected when, in fact, they are not. This is known as soldering or patching. The term comes from the process of soldering in metalwork—repairing by laying two pieces together and fusing them with liquid metal. In handwriting, however, this "repair" is visual rather than structural.

Soldered writing is generally interpreted negatively because it suggests the writer is attempting to conceal what they perceive as a flaw or mistake, trying to make the writing appear more correct than it actually is. Ironically, this effort to conceal often draws even more attention to the imperfection and makes it look worse. Unless there is a medical reason, such as *petit mal* seizures, habitual soldering indicates a tendency toward lack of integrity, dishonesty, or an unwillingness to acknowledge mistakes. In some cases there is a drug abuse issue

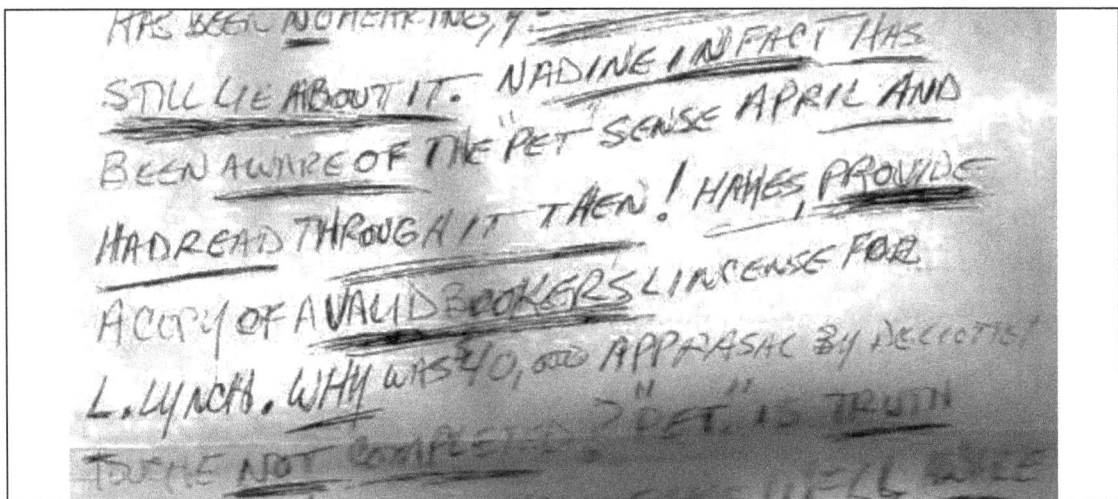

As always, context is critical. An occasional soldered letter does not mean the writer is dishonest—look at the big picture, the overall gestalt—to evaluate whether this is a consistent pattern or a rare occurrence.

When soldering is frequent or excessive, take a closer look at how often the writer employs this "patching" behavior and observe whether other red flags appear elsewhere in the handwriting.

Important clinical note

Extreme soldering—where the patching is obvious may occasionally occur in individuals with serious physiological issues. It has been observed in:

- *Heroin or other narcotics addicts, where poor memory may contribute to overwriting.*

- *Individuals experiencing petit mal seizures (absence seizures), where loses conscious for a fraction of a second, unaware they have written over an earlier stroke.*

Therefore, before assuming the worst and drawing conclusions about dishonesty, consider the possibility of underlying medical or neurological conditions.

197

Lesson Eighteen
Writing Slant

The slant or slope of handwriting refers to the angle created between the baseline and the apex of a letter where the pen turns its direction from an upstroke to a downstroke.

Slant may be seen in any of the three zones and is interpreted based on the zone in which it occurs. Regardless of where you find it, however, slant serves as a gauge of **emotional reactivity**.

- *The upslant represents movement away from the body — symbolic of the writer's immediate, instinct response (gut reaction) to emotional stimuli.*
- *The downslant returns toward the body — symbolic of the degree to which the writer expresses or restrains these emotions.*

Definition of Slant:

To give a direction other than perpendicular or horizontal to; make diagonal; cause to slope or incline diagonally.

Types of Slant

Right slant (Part of right trend)

Right trend represents movement outward—away from self, toward others. A moderate right slant reflects:

- *Warmth and empathy.*
- *Emotional openness*
- *An ability to express feelings while maintaining self-control*

The writer with the **moderate** right slant knows when to hold back and when to express emotions appropriately.

199

As the degree of slant increases, emotional responsiveness intensifies:
- *Extreme right slant may suggest over-reactivity or hysteria*
- *In such cases, upper-zone letters may nearly lie on the baseline*
- *This writer who may exhibit impulsive behavior, laughing or crying in exaggerated ways that draw attention from others*

Following are two samples with very strong right slant

200

Vertical Slant

Vertical writing does not slant in one direction or the other. It indicates emotional self-control. This writer:

- *Is more cool-headed than warm-hearted.*
- *Carefully weighs consequences before acting*
- *Maintains calm, even under stress*

Vertical writing is often accompanied by wide spatial arrangement, reflecting the writer's calm, deliberate temperament. While not unemotional, this person keeps feeling private, and is composed under most circumstances. Here are two examples.

Thought you might like a copy of our school catalogue as well. Dr. Pecci is the President and teaches classes as well as workshops.

Being with my family
Phone calls from my grandchildren
My garden in the Spring.

Left-slant

Left-slanted writing is relatively uncommon and is not, as many people believe, related to left-handedness.

- *The left-slanted writer experiences emotions as strongly as the person right-slanted writer but is emotionally protective.*

- *While friendly on the surface, long-time acquaintances may say they "don't really know him."*

The more extreme the left slant, the more the deeply feelings are hidden.

These writers may express strong opinions on external topics such as politics, movies, sports, or entertainment, but rarely expose their innermost personal feelings.

Left-slanted writing can be compared to a slingshot pulled stretched taut: tension builds as feelings are held back. When release occurs, the reaction is likely to be intense and unpredictable.

Example: The sample of Oklahoma City Bomber Timothy McVeigh a few months after his capture. The original was written in red ink.

202

Mixed Slant

The pattern of slant in handwriting indicates the writer's gut reaction to what is going on in their personal life and the environment. A recurring sequence where words begin with a leftward slant, shift to vertical, and end with are rightward slant suggests a cyclical emotional process. This signifies:

- *The leftward slant at the start reflects initial reserve, emotional distancing, or self-protection as the interaction begins.*
- *The vertical midsection shows a temporary state of emotional control or objective evaluation—a cool, calculating stance.*
- *The final rightward slant represents emotional openness, warmth, or engagement as the interaction concludes.*

However, this openness may be temporary or superficial. When the next interaction begins, the writer revers to the initial reserve, repeating the cycle. Despite outward signs of warmth, true emotional progress or intimacy may remain elusive, as the protective emotional barrier is quickly reinstated.

Here are some examples of mixed slant. Notice the varying styles that create different gestalts in each sample. In the first example, the writing is simplified in a slightly crowded picture of space.

The next sample is more of a copybook model style that is likewise slightly crowded, but projects a very different type of personality. The mixed slant may manifest differently in each.

203

Here are three writings with a great deal of variability in all areas, including slant and yet, they are quite different personalities.

life has been when my children
were small. and we did things
Together. like going to big boy
restaurant have a humburger.
in the car. or going to the Drive
in. Take a Vacation with them.

Would you Kindly
Complete Both
Sides of THE
enclosed Forms
for a Data Base.

Thank you.

attitude, I hope. Since then, all
hell has broken loose ... however
simultaneously, great opportunity
has presented itself for
International products and

204

Isolated Extreme Slant ("Maniac d")

Occasionally, a single letter within a word may show a sudden, extreme slant. While some graphologists refer to this as the "maniac d" (when seen in the letter d), it may appear in any letter. This signals:

- *Sudden, uncontrolled emotional bursts.*

- *An explosive moment of instability*

The handwriting of the Zodiac Killer, shown below, contains examples of these abrupt slant shifts on the letter *d*.

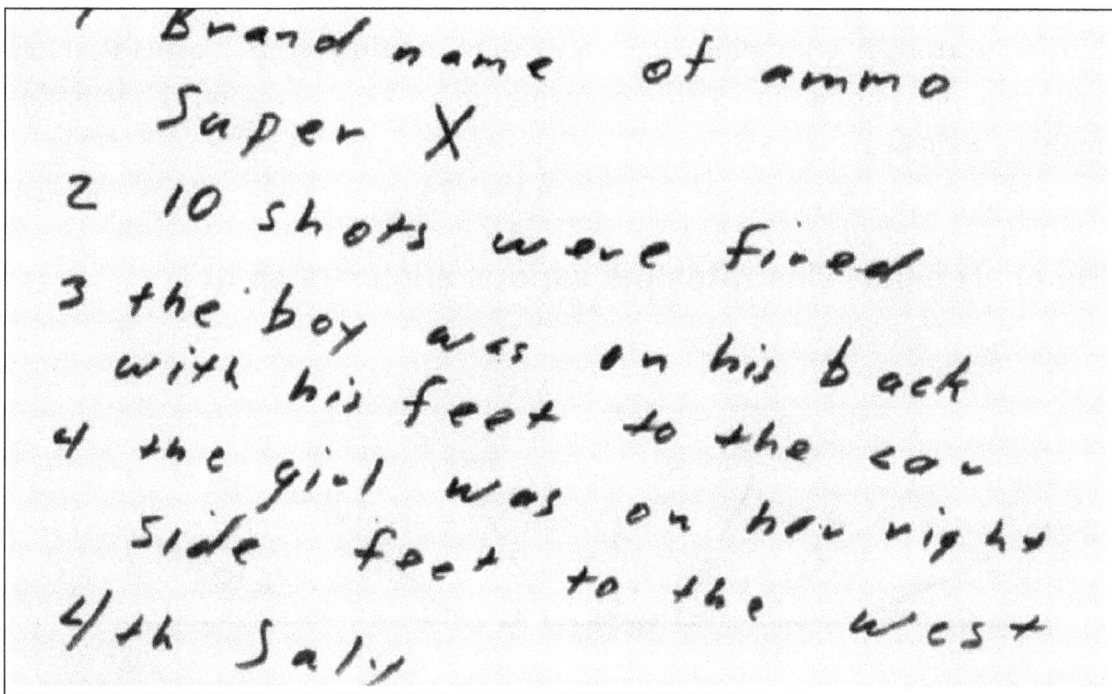

Measuring Slant

Although gestalt analysts don't usually measure handwriting, as noted previously, there are some aspects of writing that can be measured, and slant is one of them. You won't use these measurements once you are familiar with what they represent, as it will become part of your "eye training."

205

While any upper zone letter may be used to measure slant, the letter ℓ is probably the easiest.

How to Measure Slant:

1. Draw a straight line from the baseline to the top of the ℓ loop.
2. The slant angle is the acute angle formed between this line and the baseline.

Once you become familiar with the continuum of slant — extreme, strong, and moderate — and can recognize the approximate position of each, you won't need to measure the exact angle. An approximation will be sufficient for analysis. Until you develop this visual skill, however, use a protractor to measure slant accurately. A protractor can easily can be obtained from most stationary or office supply stores. Practice measuring upper loop slants on the samples you have collected.

The chart below illustrates the various angles of slant

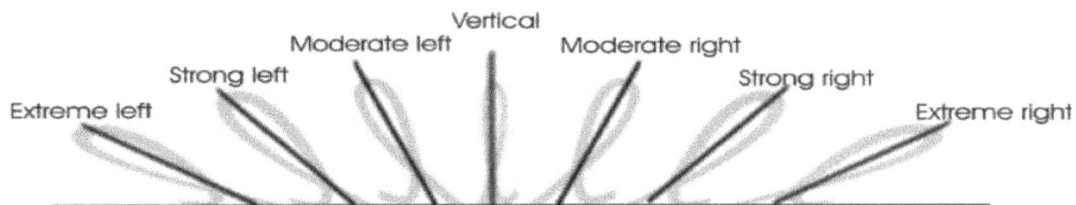

Lesson Nineteen
The Ductus

There is nothing in handwriting more fundamental than the ductus. In Gestalt graphology, ductus refers to the stroke or writing trail—the dynamic path the pen leaves on the page. The term, when borrowed from medical language, denotes a vessel that carries fluid, such as blood or lymph—literally, a duct. Similarly, in handwriting, the ductus has been compared to water flowing in a river or blood coursing through veins. It carries not only ink, but also the energy of the writer—revealing their internal rhythm, vitality, and drive.

Movement is the essence of handwriting. As we have said, without movement there is no handwriting at all—only a lifeless dot of ink. But as soon as the pen travels across the page, it leaves a visible trail that exposes aspects of the writer's inner world as clearly as a photograph of the outer appearance. By analyzing the quality of the *ductus—its flow, rhythm, and* texture—we gain valuable understanding of the writer's psyche and behavioral tendencies.

Mechanical Factors That Affect the Ductus

Several mechanical factors affect the ductus. These include:

- *Ink type*
- *Pen tip or nib design has an influence on the tactile interaction with the paper*
- *Paper type*
- *Writing surface texture*
- *How the writer holds the pen*

Effect of the Writing Instrument

When possible, it is helpful to know the type of writing instrument that was used to produce the handwriting sample. The choice of pen can give us additional insights into both the mechanics of the writing and aspects of the writer's personality.

For example, fountain pens and chisel-tipped calligraphy pens allows visible shading variations within the stroke—qualities that are largely absent with ballpoints, fiber tips, gels, or roller ball pens. The writer who selects a broad-tipped pen differs in personality traits from one who prefers a razor-sharp fine point, and these preferences show up in other aspects of the handwriting, too.

- *A long hold*
  - *grasping the barrel farther back—results in a broader stroke, especially with fountain or fiber-tipped pens.*

- *A short hold*
  - *gripping the instrument closer to the tip—positions the pen upright, producing a thinner, sharper stroke.*

- *Sharp points dig into the paper surface, creating greater friction. Writers who choose such pens tend to invite challenges and are drawn to struggle or confrontation—literal friction.*

- *Rounded or freely flowing or fiber tip pens, reflecting a preference of ease and smoother life circumstances without putting a lot of effort into it.*

The width of the stroke offers insights into the writer's relationship with comfort and pleasure:

At its core, the *ductus* refers to the quality of the ink flow—the visible trail left by the pen as it moves across the page. There are numerous way this flow can manifest, each offering information into the writer's personality. Decades ago, Dr. Rudolph Pophal categorized the ductus into three principal types—a framework that remains highly relevant today. Let's take a closer look at each type and explore how they relate to personality dynamics seen in handwriting.

Pophal Type 1. Homogeneous Ductus

Definition: Uniform in structure or composition throughout.

Appearance: The ink flows smoothly and evenly throughout the stroke, creating a warm, rich, colorful appearance.

Psychological Implications:

- *Balanced energy and emotional stability.*
- *Strong physical control.*
- *Warm, hearty, and colorful personality*
- *Often seen in conjunction with strong movement and elastic rhythm.*

Pophal Type 2. Granulated Ductus

Definition: Composed of granules; rough, uneven.

Appearance: The stroke appears grainy, dotted, or scattered under magnification, often looking weak, coarse, or blotched. May point to inconsistencies in motor coordination, tension, or strain in the writing process.

Psychological Implications:

- *Poor coping skills, prone to emotional breakdown under stress.*
- *Signs of physical tension or strain during writing.*
- *Typically found along with brittle rhythm.*

Pophal Type 3. Amorphous Ductus

Definition: Lacking definite form or shape; formless and disorganized.

Appearance: Pale, undefined, weak, and lifeless stroke.

Psychological Indications:

- *Low energy, apathy, and emotional depletion.*
- *Lacking vitality, drive, or resilience.*
- *Commonly associated with slack rhythm.*

Physical and Mental Health Affect the Stroke

The writer's physical and mental state directly affects the ductus. Physiological signs often appear in handwriting, with the edges and width of the stroke offering additional important clues about the writer's vitality, preferences, and coping mechanisms. Under strong magnification, subtle details emerge that are invisible to the naked eye.

While few graphologists are medically trained or qualified to diagnose health conditions, certain observations may raise concern. For example, the presence of tiny blobs of ink or irregularities along the ductus could indicate disruptions that, while no specifically diagnostic,might warrant the need for medical attention. In such cases, it is wise to advise to the client—**without causing alarm**—that a consultation with a healthcare professional may be appropriate for further evaluation.

Stroke Width

— *Broader strokes* suggest a preference for ease, comfort, and sensory pleasures— creature comforts hold strong appeal. However, such individuals may not always be willing to exert the sustained effort necessary to acquire these comforts.

— *Thinner strokes* reflect a greater tendency toward aesthetics, refinement, and a more restrained or ascetic approach to material gratification.

Stroke Edge

The character of the *edges* of the stroke—sharpness, pastosity, muddiness—represent a continuum, with most writers falling somewhere in the middle. Each describes not only physical features of the stroke but also distinct psychological tendencies.

Sharpness Definition:
– Having a thin edge or a fine point capable of capable of cutting or piercing.
– Clearly and distinctly set forth.

Appearance under Magnification:
– Clean and sharp, precise edges.
– Oval letters are clearly defined without blobs, blotches, or ink pooling.

Psychological implications:

— *The sharp writer has an austere, disciplined personality. They tend to be judgmental.*

— *Less drawn to sensuous pleasures, this individual experiences enjoyment through intellectual or functional accomplishment rather than indulgence in "creature comforts."*

— *The sharp stroke is consistent with a superego writing, where rigidity standards, strong self-discipline, and a highly developed conscience are evidence.*

— *Exhibits judgmental, black/white, right/wrong thinking, with little tolerance for ambiguity.*

— *Strong intellectual capacity; professions requiring precision and critical judgment are well-suited to this type: airline pilot, litigator, surgeon.*

— *Perfectionistic; imposes his harsh standards on others as well as himself; it is not easy for this type of writer to relax.*

— *Produces more linear than curved strokes, reflecting the intellectual, controlled approach to life.*

— *Highly sensitive to external stimuli. Loud noise, vulgarity, dirt, or chaos can quickly overwhelm this individual, sometimes even affecting physical well-being if exposure is prolonged.*

Important observation tip:

While sharpness is sometimes harder to assess from standard photocopies or scans, when high resolution scans are available, magnified examination of the stroke edges can still reveal these qualities.

It's difficult to tell without magnification, but the sample above is unusual, having sharpish strokes with very heavy pressure.

The sample below has medium pressure and moderately sharp stroke edges.

Margaret, Katy & I are
Going To Europe in
The Spring—; What Fun
We Will Have!

Pastosity

Definition: From Italian *pasta* — thickly applied ink, as if daubed on to the paper with a brush.

Appearance: Wide stroke with clear but softer edges; produced without heavy pressure.

Psychological Implications:

- *Easygoing personality*
- *Strong attraction to tactile and sensory experiences*
- *Long emotional memory; recalls vivid emotional experiences*
- *Enjoys rich textures, bold tastes, and artistic expression*
- *Frequently seen in artists and individuals with highly developed sensual appreciation.*

Under magnification, the edges of the stroke are clear, but lack the razor sharpness just described.

The pastose writer loves the way things feel. They are likely to stroke and touch things that attract him, whether it is fabric, skin, or something else. This individual has a long *emotional* memory and recalls emotional events vividly, in living color, as it were. Artistic people often adopt pastose writing.

The pastose writer below is **Richard Griffiths**, producer of the CNN Documentary, *Murder by Numbers*.

I decided to overcome my fears and hand-write this...
Enclosed find writing samples from four convicted serial killers!

This writing is also strongly pastose—thick, dark strokes.

interested in meeting a
enjoys outdoor activities
cultural events. a
lly accomplished at winter
skiing. a person who
their appearance and
endeavor. Jorks, are

Muddiness

At the extreme end of the stroke continuum is *muddy* handwriting. Unless, there is a known physiological issues—which should always be considered by asking the directly—the implications of this type of stroke are generally negative.

Definition: Cloudy (as with sediment), lacking luster, confused, vague.

Appearance: Heavy, blurry strokes with ink splotches in the ovals and often, ink smearing on the paper.

Psychological Implications:

- *Must be interpreted cautiously —could be the result of a physiological issue, neurological impairment, or drug use.*

- *Absent a medical cause: extreme indulgence in base desires; a lack of internal control and diminished self-restraint.*

- *Like a river swollen beyond its banks—emotions overflow uncontrollably*
- *There is no good ebb and flow of ink, which becomes more apparent when viewed under strong magnification.*

Following are two samples of muddy writing. Because there is the possibility of physiological issues, always interpret muddiness within the context of the whole writing.

The first is an example of muddiness in a person who suffered ill health due to substance abuse.

The second writer also had substance abuse issues and a very bad temper

Shading

Definition: Variations of thickness within a single stroke creating a sculptural, bas-relief effect. Found in chisel-tip pens used in calligraphy.

Appearance: Alternating thick and thin areas within individual strokes.

Psychological Implications:

- *Highly expressive personality.*
- *Seen in more artistic individuals.*
- *Rare in modern handwriting due to common use of ballpoint and fiber-tip pens..*

214

Following are two examples of shading in artistic handwriting.

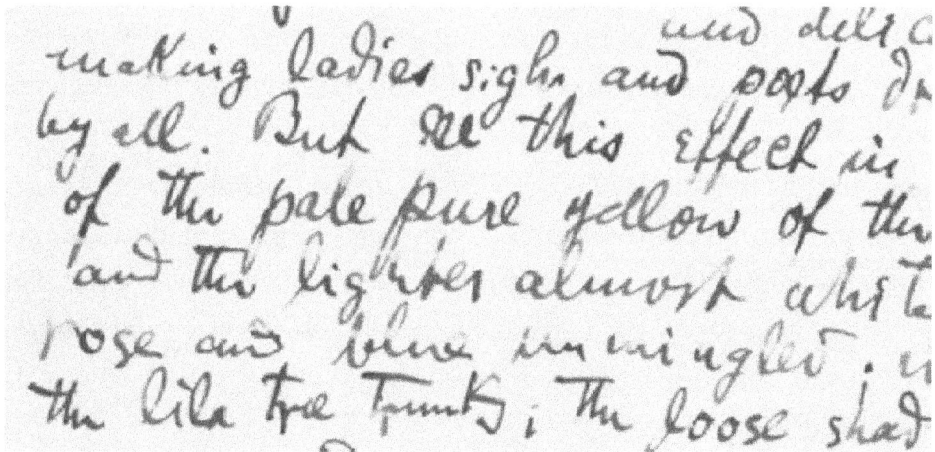

The second is calligraphy

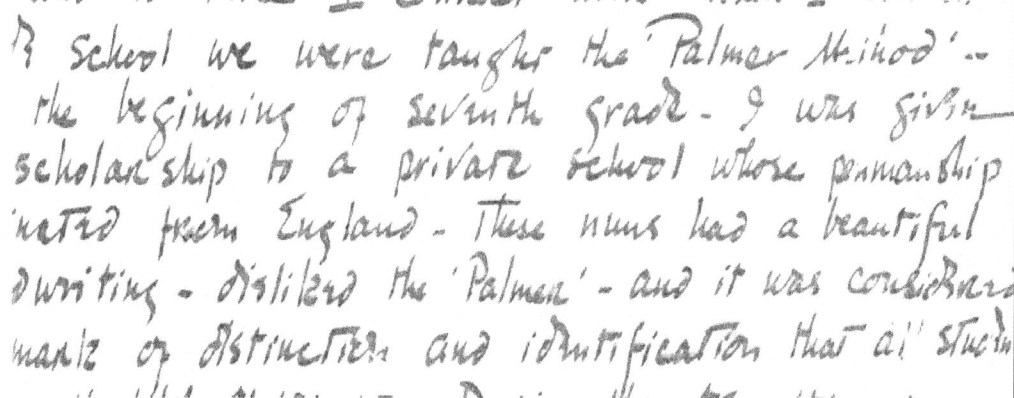

Why Studying the Ductus is Important

If you wonder why it matters that you understand the function and interpretation of the ductus, consider this: a careful study of this element adds a highly specialized but important dimension to the overall gestalt analysis of handwriting. While most elements of handwriting can be seen with the naked eye, the ductus invites us to quite literally go deeper beneath the surface to uncover fine details of both the writer's motor coordination and emotional vitality.

The ductus reveals how the writer's energy is expressed. Under strong magnification (ideally 20X or greater) the fine characteristics of the stroke can be observed to see whether the ink flows smoothly or becomes blocked or uneven. These variations can provide insight into both psychological and physical conditions.

In her seminal work *Graphology of the Stroke,* Israeli graphologist Esther Dosch delves deeply into the study of the ductus, presenting extensive high-magnification images that highlight its many subtle variations. Thanks to modern imaging technology, features once eluded early researchers are now visible in detail, making analysis a more valuable tool than ever in the study of handwriting.

Lesson Twenty
Pressure

The dictionary defines pressure *as: force applied uniformly over a surface; a mark made by application of force or weight; an impression.* In handwriting, pressure refers to the degree of force applied by the pen to the writing surface, leaving not only visual but also tactile evidence.

Pressure is intimately tied to the concept of contraction and release by the flexor and tensor muscles in the hand and their effect on the handwriting. A greater degree of contraction is often accompanied by stronger pressure; conversely, greater release tends to produce lighter pressure. Thus, pressure reflects how energy is applied or withheld as the pen moves across the page.

As always—whether excessively heavy or light pressure— extremes merits a negative interpretation.

Moderate pressure can be felt slightly on the reverse side of the page. This indicates a healthy, balanced expenditure of energy.

Very heavy pressure, which leaves braille-like ridges on the back of the paper, is a sign of frustration, and anger projected outward—towards others or the environment. When this type of pressure appears with rigid, strongly slanted writing (left or right slant), it signifies emotional tension seeking external release.

Very light pressure, while at the opposite end of the spectrum, tends to carry the same core of anger and frustration as very heavy pressure. However, it manifests differently. Instead of projecting outward, these difficult emotions are turned inward, towards the self. The result is frequently seen in depressive tendencies and self-directed anxiety.

Pressure is the depth component of handwriting

Pressure is a manifestation of mental vitality and emotional expressiveness, not physical force. While healthy, vital individuals tend to write with firm pressure, it is important to note that pressure does not directly correlate with physical strength. A large, muscular bodybuilder may write with extremely light pressure, while an eighty-year-old grandma may write with surprising firmness.

Additionally, writing speed affects pressure. Slow writing is typically accompanied by heavier pressure, while faster writing tends toward lighter pressure. This relationship which will be examined in the next section.

Three Types of Pressure

In handwriting analysis, we recognize three distinct forms of pressure, each providing valuable insight into the writer's physical, emotional, and psychological state.

1. Primary Pressure

- ***Refers to the degree to which the pen point presses into the paper.***
  - *Moderate primary pressure represents healthy vitality, stamina, and willpower.*
- *Emotional states may cause temporary shifts in pressure as the writer takes out his emotions on the paper.*
  - *Anger or excitement may lead to increased pressure as the writer subconsciously discharges emotion onto the page.*
  - *Sadness or depression may cause a temporary decrease in pressure, as diminished energy leaves the writer unable or unwilling to apply force.*
- *Because primary pressure relates to the overall energy expenditure at the moment of writing, variations often reflect transient emotional conditions as well as stable personality traits.*

2. Secondary Pressure

- *Refers to the natural alternation between light and heavier strokes as the pen moves up and down across the paper, engaging the flexor and tensor muscles of the hand. When you observe the light/heavy pattern it is normal and balanced.*

218

In a normal pressure pattern:

- *Upstrokes typically show lighter pressure than downstrokes. Upstrokes are releasing movements, directed away from the body and symbolically away from the self.*

- *Downstrokes generally show slightly heavier pressure. These movements return toward the body, symbolizing self-protective or controlling movements as they return to the body.*

- *A healthy balance between light upstrokes and firm downstrokes reflects normal muscular coordination and emotional regulation. Distortions in secondary pressure—displaced or revered pressure—generally reveal tension, emotional imbalance, or physical fatigue.*

3. Grip Pressure

- *Grip pressure refers to the degree of force applied in holding the pen itself*

- *Excessive grip pressure may lead to hand fatigue or writer's cramp, especially during prolonged writing.*

- *Overly tight grip pressure may reflect emotional rigidity, tension, or anxiety.*

- *Conversely, an abnormally loose grip may indicate passivity, low physical vitality, or disengagement.*

Displaced Pressure

As we've just described, due to a greater exertion on the pen, in a healthy pressure pattern, downstrokes carry slightly more pressure than upstrokes. This reflects the natural physiology of handwriting, where downstrokes (moving toward the body) engage the stronger flexor muscles, and upstrokes (moving away from the body) engage the weaker extensor muscles.

However—and this is more often true of *left-handed* writers—this natural pattern is displaced. In such cases, greater pressure is applied to the upstrokes or sometimes to horizontal strokes, especially on t-bars. When greater pressure consistently occurs on *upstrokes* rather than downstrokes, this is referred to displaced pressure.

Because displaced pressure represents a deviation from the body's natural motor pattern, it can be seen as a form of *deliberate* control—akin to driving a car in reverse gear. It can be done, but requires continuous, unnatural effort. Over time, this inefficient expenditure of energy is exhausting, leading to fatigue and emotional strain.

In handwriting terms, the energy is being channeled inefficiently. The writer exerts force (pushes) where there should be release (on upstrokes), and releases (lets go) where there should be control (on downstrokes). This inefficient channeling of energy reflects:

- *An ongoing struggle to control circumstances rather than allowing events to unfold naturally.*
- *A tendency toward perfectionism or rigid self-expectations.*
- *Emotional tension, internal conflict, or chronic stress.*
- *Fatigue resulting from persistent overexertion, both physical and psychological.*

As always, interpretation must take into account the zone (and the gestalt) in which **reversed pressure** appears. For example:

- *In the upper zone: mental overcontrol, worry, rigid thinking*
- *In the middle zone: emotional inhibition, strained interpersonal efforts.*
- *In the lower zone: blocked instincts, sexual tension, or compulsive behavior.*

Pushing the Pen: The Symbolism of Displaced Pressure

Handwriting is symbolic extension of human interaction: movement away from the self and toward others, followed by a return to self. In psychologically healthy individuals there is a natural rhythm and balance to this process, reflecting an ability to engage appropriately while maintaining personal boundaries.

When **reversed pressure** occurs—especially when it appears in specific zones—it signals a breakdown of this natural rhythm. Instead of allowing energy to flow outward and return smoothly, the writer exerts pressure at points where release should occur, reflecting internal tension and an excessive need for control.

The next sample, from a left-handed male in his mid-30s illustrates classic revered pressure: note the heavier upstrokes and lighter downstrokes. This writer struggles to allow life to unfold naturally, instead attempting to force situations to meet his expectations, which results in constant underlying stress.

Reversed Pressure in the Middle Zone

The **middle zone** represents day-to-day life, personal relationships, and emotional exchanges. When reversed pressure is concentrated here, the writer pushes their own thoughts, feelings, and needs onto others, often with little regard for their needs or preferences. There is an almost compulsive desire to dominate personal interactions, making others conform to their version of what is best.

The underlying driver is anxiety—a chronic need to maintain control over both self and environment. When such a writer believes their control is being threatened, they attempt literally to exert more pressure on others, pushing them to do what they believe is right for them. Control behaviors will typically also be visible elsewhere in the handwriting, in such features as:

- *Rigidity*
- *Exaggerated upper zone height*
- *Narrow middle zone*
- *Compressed or crowded spatial arrangement*

When taken together, these traits produce a negative gestalt, falling into a superego writing, which is marked by excessive self-regulation and internalized standards projected outward onto others.

Reversed Pressure in the Upper Zone

The **upper zone** represents abstract ideas, thinking, ideals, and intellectual exploration. In healthy writing:

- *The lighter upstrokes represent going out into the world, reaching out gather knowledge and experiences.*

- *The heavier downstrokes bring the information back to the self—the middle zone, the zone of reality.*

When **reversed pressure** occurs in the upper zone, the writer insists that others adopt his ideas. Arguing his position forcefully, he is often unable to tolerate opposing viewpoints until others either give up and accept his viewpoint, or they simply leave.

His main goal is not to dialogue, but to win others over to his personal set of "facts." If he perceives others as patronizing or dismissive, he is likely to react with anger and frustration. Inability to release (symbolized by the reversed pressure) feeds a persistent need to remain in control.

Reversed Pressure in the Lower Zone

The **lower zone** represents physical energy, instincts, sexuality, and the practical execution of tasks. In healthy writing, the heavier downstroke applies energy toward a goal. The lighter upstroke releases that energy as projects or relationships move forward.

When pressure is displaced into the lower zone, the writer has difficulty letting go and trusting natural processes, instead, constantly pushing for results, and feeling unable to relax into the natural flow of events. This behavior reflects a sublimation of libidinal energy, redirecting instinctual drives into ambitious, goal-oriented, or career-focused activities.

222

Summary note: *Reversed pressure, regardless of the zone, reflects a deep-seated struggle for control, a fundamental inability to release, and an internal energy that works against the natural flow of emotional and interpersonal engagement.*

This pattern of reversal in the lower zone has been observed in the handwritings of some highly successful women who channel energy into professional achievements, possibly as a compensation for emotional or sexual dissatisfaction. While effective in career pursuits, this dynamic can place strain on personal relationships.

Displacement onto the Horizontal

In normal handwriting, pressure is primarily distributed along the vertical axis—light upstrokes and heavier downstrokes reflect the natural flow of energy as the writer reaches out and returns to the self. Occasionally, however, pressure is displaced from the vertical movement and applied instead to the **horizontal axis**, and is most often observed in the form of excessively heavy, horizontal strokes, such as overemphasized t-bars.

When pressure is channeled into the horizontal this way, the writer's energy is directed outward—excessively—into ambition, achievement, and goal-seeking behavior. They place strong emphasis on gaining control, managing outcomes, and achieving success. While ambition in itself is not pathological, excessive horizontal pressure indicates an imbalance—the writer lacks the will or ability to let go and relinquish control when it is appropriate, instead, exerting sustained effort, continually pushing toward an objective, not recognizing when to stop and relax.

A Cautionary Example

We have already examined the handwriting of serial killer and rapist Robert Joseph Long, where the **horizontal strokes**—especially in **t-bars**—are a red flag for excessively controlling behavior

. Of course, this is not meant to suggest that every writer with long, strong t-crossings is dangerous. However, when you consider the gestalt—the whole picture, and you encounter many disproportionately long, heavily pressured t-bars, it should serve as a red flag for excessively controlling behavior.

Evaluating Context

When horizontal pressure is moderately strong, careful evaluation of the gestalt will provide the necessary information we need.

- *Does the writing retain enough flexibility and balance to make it unlikely the writer will misuse his control.*
- *Are there compensating signs of adaptability, emotional maturity, and healthy regulation?*
- *Or does the writing show additional signs of rigidity, compression, or suppressed emotionality?*

A writer with long, very strong t-crossings may simply be highly driven and success-oriented. But when accompanied by rigidity, tight spacing, and other signs of disturbed form or space, it signals a personality at risk for controlling, perfectionistic, or domineering tendencies.

Fluctuating Pressure

When pressure changes unpredictably from light to heavy and back to light without any regularity, it points to a disturbance in the ability to regulate energy. Such irregularity may be the result of a number of factors. Unstable energy flow may be a sign of illness or neurological impairment. Potential emotional explosiveness and unreliability are also possibilities.

This fluctuating pressure pattern is sometimes seen in the handwritings of prison inmates and violent offenders, where it indicates an ability to maintain emotional balance or self-regulation.

Or it might simply be a problem with the pen, so be cautious about drawing dire psychological conclusions.

A Case Study: Cary Stayner

A vivid example of fluctuating pressure appears in the handwriting of Cary Stayner, who brutally murdered five women in Yosemite during the 1990's.

Though written in pencil, the pressure seems to fluctuate between light and dark with no consistent pattern.

225

Stayner's personal history adds context (though never justification) to his horrific violent acts.

Cary's brother Steven was kidnapped as a seven-year-old by a pedophile. When he was 14, Steven escaped and was reunited with his family. But the tragedy didn't end there. At the age of twenty-four he died in a motorcycle accident.

Cary Stayner grew up overshadowed by this immense trauma, and according to his handwriting felt unable to fully meet his father's[1] expectations or to substitute in some way for his lost little brother.

In examining his handwriting, the eye is drawn to a **disproportionately tall upper zone,** pointing to **superego** dominance, internalized expectations, and emotional strain. The fluctuating pressure reflects deep-seated internal conflict, unresolved rage, and unstable emotional control that ultimately erupted in the worst kind of violence.

Caution!

It may be redundant, but it's important: When you observe fluctuating pressure, do not rush to interpret its meaning. First, seek additional background information regarding the writer's health. Look at the gestalt to determine whether the fluctuation is an artifact of short-term stress, emotional instability, physical illness, or something simple such as pen malfunction.

Directional Pressure

Directional pressure is not "pressure" in the traditional sense of force applied into the paper. Rather, it refers to the bending of strokes that are supposed to be straight. The concept was first introduced by Felix Klein, a handwriting analyst and Holocaust survivor. While imprisoned in the concentration camps of Buchenwald and Auschwitz during World War II, Klein discovered that inmates whose handwriting showed greater flexibility and adaptability were more emotionally resilient—and more likely to survive—than those whose handwriting remained rigid and unyielding. These subtle deviations in the stroke reflect the writer's unconscious response to extreme external stress.

---

[1] *In no way is this statement intended to blame his father. It is Cary's perception, which is not necessarily reality.

As we will see next, the direction in which the stroke bends tells the observer which area of functioning is affected.

Key Forms of Directional Pressure

Concave t-bar (bows downward) This t-bar gives the impression of being pressed down from above, symbolizing pressure from authority figures, superiors, parental expectations. It suggests the influence of someone the writer fears, respects, or feels subordinate to. See the next two samples.

The **'Felon's claw,'** mentioned in an earlier lesson, is the opposite type of directional pressure, bowing upward unnaturally. Often tied to maternal influence, it is a feeling of pressure from below, and when seen in the lower zone, sexual guilt, the result of being victimized, is present.

Following are some examples of the 'felon's claw' in different types of gestalt.

In the following sample has disturbed form, with some felons claws that show directional pressure from the right, which represents the future.

227

My mind drifted — a picture formed of
Ourselves — and I listened to brief words
spoken by you. Looking into your EYES,
I smiled.
+E day is now night. Reading your words,

In the lower zone, where downstrokes should descend vertically, you may observe strokes bending to the left. This is directional pressure from the right, symbolizing apprehension, or tension about what lies ahead.

Both fluctuating pressure and directional pressure reveal subtle but important aspects of how the writer processes internal and external pressures. While fluctuating pressure reflects the writer's difficulty in regulating emotional energy, directional pressure shows how the writer adapts (or fails to adapt) to external stressors and demands.

Loops bent inward from the left signifies pressure from the past. Note: in some cases, it may be an indicator of spinal damage, depending on medical context.

Brien you are a cool person
I must say you really are
ep person. I really enjoy your
of thinking. Hand writing or
in general really motivat
mind and expressions. I oft

Loop bent inward from the right are symbolic of feelings of pressure or anxiety about the future, what is coming next, or expectations.

Measuring Pressure

In the early days of modern graphology, specialized instruments were developed to measure pressure, but these devices are no longer in use today. Over time, several low-tech methods have been suggested, though most are impractical.

One such method involved inserting layers of carbon paper between sheets of writing paper. The number of carbon sheets the handwriting penetrated was used as a crude measure of pressure. While this technique could yield useful information, it is cumbersome and rarely applied in modern practice.

For most purposes, a simple tactile examination of the reverse side of the paper is sufficient. Turn the paper over and run your fingers over the reverse side of the writing. If you can feel the writing very slightly embossed on the other back, the pressure is moderate. If the writing produces deep indentations that are like braille, almost tearing the paper, the pressure is extreme. If there is no impression at all, the pressure is light.

Evaluating Pressure Without Originals

Historically, many graphologists adhered to a strict policy of analyzing only original handwriting samples, viewing copies as inadequate for accurate assessment. While this stance was once considered essential, it is largely impractical in today's professional landscape. In fields such as employment screening,

229

psychological assessment, and forensic examination, originals are seldom available, and timely results are critical. As a result, high-quality copies have become an accepted and necessary alternative.

While original documents are ideal, in most cases, modern technology make it possible to conduct accurate evaluations using digital photographs or high-resolution scans. A 300 dpi color scan or photo can often provide sufficient detail for a skilled graphologist to assess the writing effectively.

Photocopies and faxes are less desirable, as they can distort fine details such as line quality, pressure, and ductus. However, an experienced graphologist can usually compensate for these limitations. Adjusting the copier or scanner, or making adjustments in graphics editing software, can reveal subtle variations in pressure by increasing the visibility of tonal contrast across the writing.

You won't be able to detect the actual physical pressure of the writing without the original, but sometimes the light/dark patterns can be better detected on a photocopy. Careful visual and tactile evaluation—combined with technological tools—allows for meaningful analysis even when originals are unavailable.

Lesson Twenty-One
Speed

Speed is defined as "the rate at which an object covers distance, essentially measuring how fast something is moving." In handwriting analysis, the speed at which a text is written tells a lot about the way a person thinks, feels, and approaches life. A writer who processes information quickly and reacts swiftly to emotional stimuli is unlikely to produce plodding, slow handwriting. Conversely, the writer who thinks methodically and processes information at a measured pace will produce slower handwriting.

Since handwriting serves the purpose of communication, when it comes to evaluating speed, *legibility* plays a key role. If the writing is sloppy, careless, and illegible, it may suggest underlying hostility or, at a minimum, a lack of consideration for the reader. Barring physical or cognitive impairment, turning in illegible writing reflects a lack of regard for the recipient and borders on rudeness.

Extremely thready writing is fast, and in this case, legibility is impacted. The test is whether you can take a word out of context and read it easily.

The **fast writer** processes information quickly and acts quickly, adapting to circumstances as they change. This writer is often intuitive, able to grasp new ideas and concepts rapidly, applying them effectively in practical situations.

The next writing is fast and has thread, but not to the point of illegibility.

The faster the writing, the less the writer is willing to delay gratification. Highly rapid writing indicates impulsivity, and impatience. This writer does not suffer fools gladly and insists on rapid results.

This is fast, dynamic writing

Impulsiveness can send the writer diving into a situation without adequate forethought, sometimes leading to unintended consequences. Routine work that demands sustained attention to detail quickly becomes tedious. The writer can be described as an "action junkie" who thrives on movement and change rather than sedentary or repetitive tasks. Always seeking novelty and simulation, interacting with people who process information more slowly may irritate him, and his impatience is apt to be evident in his behavior.

At the extreme, the too-fast writer, as in the thready writing we saw earlier, is impulsive to a fault. His decisions may be rash, leading to serious difficulties. Nervous energy drives much of his behavior, and he may seek constant activity not for meaningful accomplishment but as a way of self-soothing or distracting himself from inner restlessness. For this writer, movement becomes a tranquilizer rather than a path to productivity.

A very fast writer is unhappy at a routine desk job. He seeks opportunities to go out and about, seeking new adventures. Annoyed by those who are slower thinkers, he is likely to show his impatience when they can't keep up.

The following two samples are medium-slow speed, due to the large size in the first example and careful form in the second.

233

The gestalt is slightly disturbed due to the elaboration, however there is enough simplification in this sample to designate it as medium speed.

This letter is to give you written notice of the end of my tenancy as required by the terms of our rental agreement. The premises at 18 B Williams Street, Williamsburg, MA 01096 shall be vacant, broom clean and available on May 01, 2014.

The next sample was written slowly due to physiological issues.

for depression. I wanted to thank you for CD player. I love it. I use it every night to help me go to sleep. It was so nice of you to think of me. My mom talks about you often.

This sample is slow due to the size and elaborations.

How are you, I am fine. You dropped by we talked about you were a nightmare to I said I could understand. Have a Nice Day

234

Fast and slow writing have a different set of characteristics to identify them. A writing doesn't need to contain *all* of these to qualify for fast.

Medium-speed writing falls between the two extremes.

Characteristics of Fast Writing

- *Good rhythmic flow*

- *Simplification of form*

- *Connected (but not over-connected)*

- *Some primary thread*

- *Moderate pressure*

- *Wide, but not too wide, spaces between words*

- *Slightly rising and/or slightly wavy baseline*

- *Thready endings of letters or words*

- *Fast arcade connections in the upper zone*

- *Missing initial and final strokes*

- *i dots that move to the right of the stem*

- *i dots that look like dashes or tent-shaped*

- *Moderate right slant*

- *Rightward tending margins*

- *i dots and t bars connecting to the next letter*

- *Some straight lower zone downstrokes at ends of words*

- *No exaggerations, such as extra-long upper or lower zone lengths, elaborate capitals; no extremes in size, either large or small.*

Slow Writing

Extremes in writing contribute to a slowing of speed. For example, handwriting that is very large size, or one that is highly regular naturally reduce velocity, even if the writer's cognitive speed is otherwise adequate.

At its most extreme, very slow writing may signal intellectual and/or emotional underdevelopment, or the effects of external influences such as heavy

235

medication. In such cases, the sluggish pace reflects a diminished ability to process information or respond promptly to environmental demands. The slow writer is methodical and pragmatic in his approach, preferring to carefully examine all available facts and data before making decisions. Trusting logic over intuition, this writer is typically cautious, resisting being rushed or pressured into action before he feels fully prepared. He is less inclined to venture into uncharted territory or generate entirely new ideas, instead, finding comfort and security within his established routines and familiar social circle.

Characteristics of slow writing

- *High attention to detail (e.g., precise I dots and t crosses, careful punctuation)*
- *High degree of connectedness*
- *Strong organization*
- *Tight or rigid rhythm*
- *Straight of falling baseline*
- *Retains initial and final strokes*
- *Looped and/or intruded ovals*
- *Many angular forms*
- *Many careful arcade forms*
- *Narrowing margins*
- *Narrow word and letter spacing*
- *Middle zone narrower than tall*
- *Squeezed or retraced upper and/or lower loops*
- *Very large upper and or lower loops*
- *Many elaborations*

Interacting with his opposite—the fast writer—can create tension as he becomes frustrated when forced to keep pace with someone who moves and thinks more rapidly. He performs best when given time and space to work at his own deliberate speed, free from the pressure of someone leaning over his shoulder, supervising. Stability is important to this writer; a consistent environment and predictable routine allow him to function at his highest capacity.

As we come to the end of the lessons on space, form, and movement, the following quote seems apropos. Just substitute the word "movement" for "energy"

"Everything in this world is made of energy...Since energy is actually vibration, that means that everything that exists vibrates...."

Modern-day physicists have finally come to agree that energy and matter are one and the same, which brings us back to where we started: that everything vibrates, because everything—whether you can see it or not—is energy.

Pure, pulsing, ever-flowing energy......energy vibrates differently. Just like the sound that pours out of a musical instrument, some energy vibrates fast (such as high notes) from high frequencies, and some vibrates slow (such as low notes) from low frequencies.

Unlike the tones from a musical instrument, however, the energy that flows out from us comes from our highly charged emotions to create highly charged electromagnetic wave patterns of energy, making us powerful—but volatile—walking magnets."

Lynne Grabthorne

237

PART FOUR

Putting it all Together

Lesson Twenty-Two
Time to Review

Students of Gestalt graphology must first learn the building blocks that comprise each of the three major dimensions of handwriting: space, form, and movement. You have now done that work. Once those indicators and their basic meanings become second nature and you fully understand each of those components, the whole picture begins to emerge naturally. The writing is no longer a collection of separate features—it becomes a cohesive structure

The Building Blocks *Are* the Building

In Parts One—Space, Two—Form, and Three—Movement, we explored numerous graphic indicators and assigned each a general meaning with the understanding that those meanings must be adjusted within the context of the overall writing. To recognize the core personality—the true individual behind the handwriting—we must interpret space, form, and movement together as a unified whole.

As you now know, one of the basic tenets of gestalt graphology is this: meanings can and do change depending on context. There is no "this means that" definition which applies universally. The whole is different from the sum of its parts

---

You may have heard the ancient tale of the blind men and the elephant, which applies directly to our approach.

A group of blind men, curious about a strange animal they had never seen, decided that each would touch it to determine its nature.

- — *The first one felt the trunk and said it was a snake.*
- — *The second felt its ear and thought it was a fan.*
- — *The third touched the leg called it a tree trunk.*
- — *The fourth, feeling its side, described it as a wall.*
- — *The fifth man grasped the tail and it a rope.*
- — *The last man touched the tusk and concluded it was a spear.*

Each correctly described the individual part they examined, but their inability to perceive the whole hindered their interpretation of what they had found and led to inaccurate conclusions. In handwriting analysis, the same danger exists when only isolated features are considered. Describing the tusk as hard and smooth was correct, but concluding it was a spear was not. Accurate interpretation requires an awareness of the entire personality structure reflected in the writing.

To underscore this point, let's take an example from the trait-stroke method: so-called resentment strokes—straight strokes at the beginnings of words, rising from below the baseline—like the sample below.

In trait-stroke analysis, these strokes are said to always signify resentment from the past. But that information is incomplete. It tell us nothing about the origin of the resentment or how manifests in the writer's life. In this case, it doesn't tell you that the writer overcame a difficult background to become a highly skilled psychotherapist who helped turn around the lives of many clients. A simple list of personality trait names, without a contextual synthesis, is not sufficient to properly understand the person and how they operate.

242

Seeing the Whole First

Using the gestalt method, you begin by absorbing the entire picture of space, form, and movement. Rather than zooming in and focusing on isolated features like "resentment strokes," you step back and take in the overall impression of the writer—*the gestalt*. Your first task is to evaluate whether the gestalt is balanced or disturbed, and if there is an imbalance, to determine which of the three major dimensions—space, form, or movement, is responsible.

Only after this global evaluation do you begin to look closer and examine the smaller elements. At this stage, you may observe certain straight (linear) strokes at the beginnings of words. Rather than automatically labeling them "resentment strokes," the Gestalt analyst recognizes these rigid strokes rising from below the baseline—the subconscious—into the middle zone area of everyday functioning. Their meaning is not fixed. Depending on what appears elsewhere in the spatial arrangement, letter forms, and writing movement, you interpret how these strokes fit into the specific personality reflected in the handwriting.

As master graphologist Edward B. O'Neill explained, the trait-stroke method is like viewing handwriting through a microscope, which has a very small field of vision. You would see the writing only bit by bit on the viewing platform, and would have to construct a personality profile one piece at a time. Gestalt analysis, on the other hand, is like viewing handwriting through a telescope, seeing the whole all at once. Both approaches have their merits.

If you are still finding it difficult to see the big picture, don't be discouraged. Gestalt graphology is a complex area of study that requires experience, repetition, and a lot of practice, which means the careful examination of a large number of handwriting samples over time.

This process seems to come more easily to naturally right-brained, conceptual thinkers who are more inclined to "see the building" rather than focus on the individual building blocks.

Highly analytical, left-brained thinkers may find the Gestalt approach challenging at first, as they are more comfortable dealing with discrete details. But with time and dedication, even the most detail-oriented student can learn to

243

shift perspective and appreciate the richness that Gestalt analysis offers. As they discover a different way of seeing, they find it is worth the effort.

Refining the Analysis

To extend the building block analogy one step further, after recognizing what kind of building you are looking at—whether it's an elaborate mansion, a charming cottage, a ranch-style home, or a broken-down hovel—it becomes important to examine the building materials from which it is constructed.

By now, you may be tired of hearing that in Gestalt analysis, meanings of individual indicators are always relative and must be verified, modified, or neutralized by other indicators in the perceptual field, and that heir significance depends on where they appear within the dimensions of space, form, or movement.

Hopefully, you are ready move toward synthesizing your findings into a written analysis.

Two of my books—*Reading Between the Lines: Decoding Handwriting* and *Succeeding in the Business of Handwriting Analysis*—both included with this course, offer detailed guidance on writing an analysis. Rather than repeat information here, the following lesson introduces an important aspect of personality that can serve as a useful starting point for your analysis: *Motivation and Drives.*

Lesson Twenty-Three
Typologies

Felix Klein, widely considered a major figure in modern graphology, frequently advised, *"If you know the* type, *you know everything."* He incorporated several personality typologies into his work, including those developed by Erich Fromm, Alfred Adler, and others.

In my own practice, I have found two typological systems especially helpful:

— *The 16 Myers-Briggs (Jungian) types and*

— *The 9 Enneagram types.*

There is no shortage of excellent resources available about these systems. You will find numerous books, articles, and videos online. I recommend starting with *The Enneagram Made Easy*, and *Type Talk*. Another valuable reference is *Personality Self-Portrait,* which references the personality types detailed in the Diagnostic and Statistical Manual used by mental health professionals.

Once you become familiar with the basic structure and descriptions of these personality types, you can begin applying them to handwriting analysis. As you recognize clusters of indicators in the handwriting that correspond to specific type patterns, you will find yourself able to construct highly accurate personality portraits.

Flexibility in Using Typologies

Some people object to using typologies, claiming they attempt to squeeze people into a box. But here's the thing: few people fit neatly into any pure type. Once you recognize a general type that seems to fit the handwriting, you can take what applies, consider the influence of a secondary type, and disregard

245

anything that doesn't fit. With the Enneagram, for example, not only do you have the nine basic types to call on, but also wings and arrows that add further nuance and flexibility.

Following is a very brief summary of the basic nine Enneagram types and some general handwriting characteristics associated with each. Keep in mind, this is only a starting point. There is far more to learn about both the personality types and their handwriting correlates.

Enneagram Quick Reference

Type One – The Perfectionist.

Personality: Detail-minded, self-critical, and highly aware of flaws in self and of others. Feels a strong need to suppress anger, to be "good" and do good. Hardworking, serious, practical, highly responsible, gets things done.

Handwriting: Predominance of straight lines with angles, well-organized spatial arrangement, narrow letter width, possible upper zone emphasis, tight, controlled rhythm.

Type Two – The Helper

Personality: Needs to be needed in order to feel worthy of love. Generous, attentive to others' needs, but neglectful of their own. Resentment builds up if unappreciated.

Handwriting: More curves than straight lines, compact spatial arrangement, emphasis on the middle and sometimes lower zones, right slant, may have strong regularity.

Type Three – The Achiever.

Personality: Hardworking, identifies with their career choice. Charismatic, image-conscious, driven to succeed. Fears failure and strives for recognition. Energetic and enthusiastic, motivational.

Handwriting: Medium to large size, swinging rhythm, rightward trend, well-developed lower zone, often features a showy or attention-getting signature.

246

Type Four – The Individualist (Nonconformist)

Personality: Deeply sensitive, creative, and introspective. Feels a deep need to be unique, but with a strong fear that no one can ever understand them. Spends a great deal of time analyzing his feelings. Regularly falls into dark moods, can experience mood swings and period of melancholy.

Handwriting: Released rhythm, tasteful elaboration, artistic capitals, strong right slant, wide word spacing, pastosity, aesthetically pleasing appearance; variability, long lower zone.

Type Five – The Investigator

Personality: Intellectual, highly sensitive, 'absentminded professor.' May have strong feelings, but tends to withdraw into the realm of abstract thought. Social skills not well-developed, prefers deep thinking over social interaction.

Handwriting: Small overall size, narrow, frequently manuscript printing, wide spatial arrangement, upper zone emphasis, typically lighter pressure.

Type Six – The Loyalist

Personality: Cautious, finds it hard to trust others, but loyal once trust is earned. Feels insecure, worries about potential dangers. Good at troubleshooting, but lacks spontaneity. Some sixes, however, are counterphobic and become aggressive and anti-authority, risk-taking.

Handwriting: Narrow, angular writing, upper zone emphasis, heavier pressure, compact space (or very wide space); round, carefully placed i dots. Sometimes middle zone neglect.

Type Seven – The Enthusiast

Personality: Lively and extroverted, always looking for the next best thing. Restless, easily bored, prone to overindulgence, often addicted to substances or activities (shopping, gambling, etc.). Self-denial or gratification delayed is not an option. Good self-promoters and networkers but difficulty focusing for long periods or sticking with commitments.

Handwriting: Loose, variability, active rhythm, fast, strong rightward trend.

Type Eight – The Challenger

Personality: Forceful and highly assertive. Insists on being in control. Strong-willed, tough-minded, willing to do be the bad guy. Fiercely protective of loved ones. Powerful physical appetites. Guards against being taken advantage of. Rough-tough language, leads with chin and won't back down.

Handwriting: Heavy pressure, possibly muddy or sharp or a combination, right slant, angles, strong rightward trend, long lower zone. Block print.

Type Nine – The Peacemaker

Personality: Easygoing, goes with the flow, conflict-avoidant. Optimistic, believes things will somehow just work out. Warm and attentive, seeks harmony and connection with others. Drawn to nature, animals, small children, peaceful environments.

Handwriting: Rounded forms, highly connected, pastose, medium pressure, right slant and trend, compact spatial arrangement.

Wrapping up

This brief outline of the Enneagram types is simply to demonstrate just one way typologies can enhance your handwriting analysis. Of course, there is far more depth to both the personality descriptions and their handwriting indicators. That is part of your continuing study.

Now, let's turn to another important starting place—what makes the writer tick at a glance.

Lesson Twenty-Four
Motivations

Now that you've thoroughly explored the elements that comprise the gestalt in handwriting—those features that comprise space, form, and movement—a valuable starting point for any analysis is the writer's basic motivation. As we've just seen in the discussion of personality typologies, understanding what motivates a person means that you already have a lot of information and insight into their core needs, drives, and behaviors.

The forms and shapes found in handwriting, and the relative emphasis (or lack thereof) in any of those major dimensions—space, form, or movement—offer important clues to the writer's emotional and intellectual development. They also point to what compels or restricts the writer in life.

Motivation: *the psychological feature that arouses an organism to action toward a desired goal; the reason for the action; that which gives purpose and direction to behavior.*

Adding to that definition, motivation can also be viewed as the drive to meet one's needs—either by taking action and moving toward a desired outcome, or away from an undesired one. Whether driven by aspiration or avoidance, motivation shapes behavior in powerful ways.

There are many models of motivation in psychology, but one of the most widely recognized and easily applied is Maslow's Hierarchy of Needs, first introduced in 1954. This model continues to influence psychological theory and lends itself well to handwriting analysis.

Maslow described a five-tier pyramid of human needs, ranging from basic survival to the pursuit of personal growth and fulfillment. According to his theory, individuals move through these stages as their lower-level needs are met. However, progress is not always linear—it's never a matter of 'getting there' and that's all there is to it; life events may cause someone to regress to a lower level of need before they move forward again.

The Five Levels of Maslow's Hierarchy

1. **Physiological Needs** — Food, water, shelter
2. **Safety Needs** — Security, stability
3. **Love and Belonging Needs** — Family, friendship, intimacy, acceptance in a group
4. **Esteem Needs** — Recognition, respect, self-worth
5. **Self-Actualization Needs** — Fulfillment of potential, morality, creativity

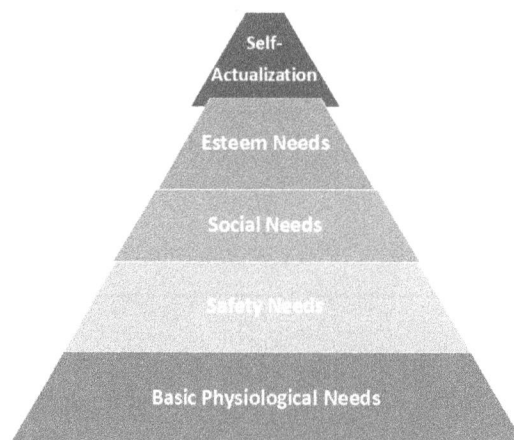

At the top of the pyramid is self-actualization—the level at which a person has become fully realized and functions with a strong sense of purpose, ethics, and authenticity. Maslow believed self-actualized individuals were motivated not by deficiency, but by growth, a strong sense of personality responsibility, and ethics. He cited examples such as Abraham Lincoln, Thomas Jefferson, Albert Einstein, Eleanor Roosevelt, and Jane Addams. It might be worth not-

250

ing that no one is entirely "self-actualized" or without flaws. Jefferson was a slave owner; Einstein cheated on his wife, etc.—human complexity persists at all levels of development You don't have to be "all good" to be self-actualized.

Discussions and handwriting examples of these and other individuals Maslow identified as self-actualized can be found in my book, *Advanced Studies in Handwriting Psychology*.

Maslow's Hierarchy: How Motivations Shape Behavior

Maslow proposed that all humans experience a common set of needs, beginning with the most basic—food, water, air—without which we cannot survive. Unless these physiological needs are met, an individual cannot effectively progress to the so-called higher needs. His theory suggests that once a level of need is fulfilled, the person naturally shifts focus to the next level up. At any given time, individuals are focused on the level that is most pressing in their lives.

Some individuals may remain at a lower level of the hierarchy for their entire lives. Someone living in a refugee camp is likely to be wholly preoccupied with securing food and water for themselves and their children. In such a situation, higher needs like self-esteem or creativity have little relevance—survival takes precedence.

Similarly, for someone who has attained a higher level experiences a sudden catastrophe such as a natural disaster, or a violent attack, their focus immediately returns to the most basic concern: staying alive. They're not thinking about next week's baseball game or long-term career goals. They are focused on taking their next breath.

Consider the impact of losing your job and having no idea how you'll afford your next meal or the mortgage or rent. Are you going to worry about what's playing at the local theater or plan for self-actualization? Hardly. Your energy is once again directed at securing shelter, food, and safety for yourself and your loved ones. This shift highlights the second level of Maslow's hierarchy—safety and security needs.

Needs Levels and Handwriting

Handwriting tells us how a person is operating on the hierarchy of needs. Someone stuck at the bottom tier, still struggling to meet basic physiological needs, may show undeveloped, rudimentary (uneducated) handwriting. Such individuals rarely seek the services of a handwriting analyst, as they're consumed by basic survival.

Therefore, in our work, we typically begin with the **second level**: concerns about safety, security, and stability. These needs are often reflected in handwriting that displays tension, rigidity, or excessive control. In contrast, writers operating at higher levels—such as belonging, esteem, or even self-actualization—tend to exhibit broader, freer, and more expressive writing styles.

As you move forward with your analysis, understanding the writer's motivational level will help you contextualize the space, form, and movement you observe. A seemingly "negative" trait may be a coping mechanism shaped by urgent unmet needs, and not necessarily a sign of pathology.

Need Level 2: Safety & Security

> **Safety**: *Freedom from risk or danger; safety*

> **Security**: *Freedom from doubt, anxiety, or fear; confidence*

The second level of Maslow's hierarchy concerns the general need for stability, protection, and predictability. This need can show up in many ways—from the desire to walk down the street without fear of being mugged, to the more routine necessity of having a stable job and regular paycheck. The focus here is on the latter: *material and emotional stability*.

The person stuck operating at this level feels most secure when all the bills are paid well in advance, the pantry is fully stocked, insurance coverage is more than sufficient, and there is plenty of money in the bank. And even then, there is the persistent nagging worry—what if it's not enough? The focus remains on safeguarding him and his family from uncertainty.

Because of this mindset, these individuals often seek out traditional employment where they can count on a steady paycheck. They are typically conserva-

252

tive and conventional in both lifestyle and values. In relationships, they function within well-known roles and routines, preferring the familiar to the unpredictable. Anything outside their lived experience may feel threatening.

Handwriting Characteristics of Level 2

As in all the levels, there is, of course, a range—from the writer who will do anything to make sure that he is safe and secure—to the person who is more balanced. Writers operating from this level often show:

- *"Squared" forms—the strong use of arcades (arched connection)—which symbolically represent a protective shelter under which the writer can psychologically retreat. This includes some forms of block printing as below.*

- *Strokes that consistently return to the baseline reflect a strong need to stay grounded and stable.*

- *The overall gestalt is good—spatial arrangement is overly wide, but within balance.*

- *Movement is strong. It may lack speed but has integrity.*

The block printed handwriting sample below represents a mid-point of Level 2

As discussed in the lesson on rhythm, good rhythm results from a healthy balance of contraction and release. In a sample where contraction dominates, with very little release, it produces a squeezed, contracted appearance and is a sign of fear—in this case, fear of scarcity or insufficiency.

The writer of the next sample carefully returns to the baseline with every letter. Symbolically, this represents a deep need to "keep their feet on the ground." There is an unconscious fear that without this stability, they may "float away and be lost." Sticking closely to copybook forms reflects the tendency to stick with the known, rarely branching out into unfamiliar territory.

Level 3: Needs for Love, Affection & Belonging

To be a part of something or someone else

Level 3 of Maslow's hierarchy centers on overcoming loneliness and fulfilling the need to love and be loved. This includes both giving and receiving affection, and finding a sense of belonging within a group—whether that group is family, a religious community, a workplace, or social organization.

Handwriting Characteristics of Level 3 Needs

Roundedness in handwriting is one of the clearest signs that the writer is emotionally expressive and capable of love. As always, balance is key: a mature, well-developed individual shows a healthy mixture of rounded and straight strokes. But when roundedness is extreme and dominant, it signals a writer stuck at this level, still seeking affection, attention, and approval in ways that can be self-defeating or excessive.

254

This is often seen in individuals who experienced abuse, neglect, or emotional deprivation in childhood. The adult who did not receive the love and support they needed during formative years may continue to long for it with great intensity—always seeking, but never feeling fully satisfied.

Case Example: Level 3 Writer

The following handwriting sample belongs to a 33-year-old, left-handed woman who reported an abusive childhood with an alcoholic father. Her mother died of cancer during her teenage years, leaving her to assume the role of caregiver for her younger half-siblings.

As an adult, she exhibits a deep need for love and emotional support. She married a military man who, despite his strengths, is emotionally distant—unable to provide the affection she craves (he is a block printer). Subconsciously, she attaches herself to older women whom she treats as mother substitutes, lavishing them with gifts and attention in a bid to feel loved and accepted.

In her handwriting, the forms are excessively rounded rather than balanced between curved and linear strokes. Her handwriting reflects the emotional hunger of someone caught at this motivational level.

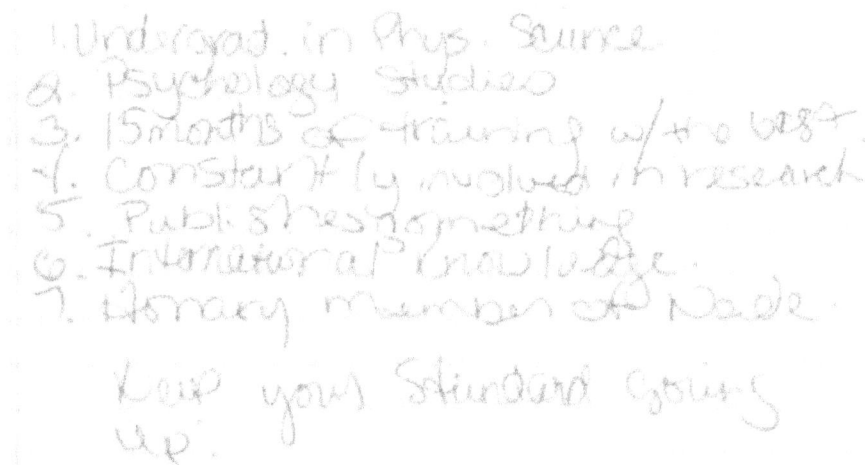

Extremes of any kind diminish balance, and in this case, the overuse of curves disrupts the harmony of the gestalt.

Nicole Brown Simpson: An Even More Extreme Case

A portion of Nicole Brown Simpson's handwriting, as shown in Lesson Nine and below, offers a dramatic illustration of Level 3 fixation. The forms are excessively rounded, departing slightly from copybook but weak due to imbalance of virtually no straight strokes.

The spatial arrangement is crowded overall, which further weakens the writing, and the movement is slow, contributing to an overall weak gestalt. When viewed as a whole, the imbalance across space, form, and movement is immediately apparent. Something feels "off," and that something is the absence of internal balance.

Nicole Brown Simpson

Too much roundedness in handwriting symbolizes a need to be literally encircled—to be surrounded by love, affection, attention, and approval. A person stuck at this level may go to extremes to get these needs met. For example, they may dress in attention-getting ways, even while claiming they don't want the kind of attention it draws. The contradiction itself becomes part of the behavioral pattern.

256

This individual may also overeat, drink excessively, overspend, over-talk—anything to buffer the emotional void they experience. Like the person stuck at level 2 never feels financially secure, the person stuck at Level 3 never feel emotionally secure. No matter how much love or attention they receive, it never seems to be enough.

Level 4 Needs - Esteem, Self-Respect & Respect of Others

To feel or show deferential regard for; esteem; to regard highly; think much of

Level 4 in Maslow's hierarchy centers on the human need for self-esteem and the esteem of others. When this level is satisfied, the individual feels confident, competent, and valuable. However, when these needs go unmet, the person feels inferior, weak, helpless, or unworthy—often resulting in compensatory behaviors or exaggerated self-presentation.

Handwriting Indicators of Level 4 Needs

A striking example of these dynamics can be seen in the handwriting of Jacqueline Kennedy Onassis in the following sample.

Jacqueline Kennedy

257

- *The overly tall capitals and disproportionately tall upper zone are less common in a woman's handwriting and suggest a pronounced need for esteem—both self-respect and respect from others.*

- *The linear quality of the writing form reveal an independent nature, more aligned with traditionally masculine traits of the era. The restrained, almost stoic appearance and left slant reflect a deliberate effort to contain emotion, perhaps because the emotions at the time were too painful to face—the letter is dated not long after the assassination of her husband.*

- *The disproportionately tall capitals—simple but elegant—when compared to the middle zone height, implies a disconnect between the ideal self and the real self. The writer may have high aspirations or internal ideals that do not feel attainable or matched by her lived experience (her history shows us something other than what she may have felt).*

Despite these indicators of inner conflict, the overall gestalt of the handwriting is good:

- *the spatial arrangement is clear and well-organized*

- *The form is simplified in a positive way—deviating thoughtfully from copybook and showing individuality and originality.*

- *The movement is slightly disturbed due to a lack of forward impetus. There is insufficient drive in the writing's progression, which subtly communicates **emotional** hesitancy or internal constraint.*

Level Five Needs - The Self-Actualized Person

According to Maslow, only after all the lower-level needs are met can a person truly ascend to the highest level: *self-actualization*. At this stage, an individual becomes free to do what they were born to do—to live authentically and create what Maslow called "peak experiences."

This means that if someone is a natural musician, they will make music because they must. If they are a writer, they write out of an inner compulsion. The self-actualized person does not seek external validation for their actions; they are internally driven, doing what fulfills them on a deep and personal level.

In contrast, the person who is not self-actualized often feels unsettled, agitated, restless, or unfulfilled—as if something essential is missing. They may appear successful from the outside, but inside they know they are not living in alignment with their potential.

Maslow's model does not easily account for the archetypal "starving artist" who sacrifices comfort or even safety in pursuit of personal expression. In such cases, we might ask: Did this person bypass lower needs to reach self-actualization? Or is that person still operating within the lower levels while grasping for the highest?

Unlike the earlier levels—where needs like food, shelter, safety, and belonging are readily observable—self-actualization is highly individual. One person may reach this level through scientific research; another through community service, spiritual practice, or artistic expression, etc.

Self-actualization may not be essential for survival, but it is often vital for inner peace and a deep sense of fulfillment.

What does the handwriting of the self-actualized person look like?

There is no single "look" to the handwriting of a self-actualized person. Like all other personality expressions, it can take many forms. However, certain common characteristics do emerge when we study the handwriting of those Maslow considered self-actualized.

Generally, we find:

- *A good gestalt — the writing appears well-balanced and cohesive at first glance.*
- *Simplified forms — no need to impress or overdecorate.*
- *Writing that reflects authenticity, confidence, and emotional integration.*

Another powerful example is Dean Koontz, the bestselling author whose books have sold over a half-billion copies (that's *billion* with a 'B'). His handwriting, shown next, demonstrates:

- *A strong gestalt.*
- *Balanced, warm (pastose), and confident strokes*
- *Strong form and fluid movement, doesn't draw attention to itself.*

While the spatial arrangement is slightly crowded (which *in this gestalt* suggests strong internal energy in one who gets things done), the overall impres-

sion is one of psychological health and well-integrated personality traits.

Koontz' life story adds further context. Before a high school teacher intervened and set him on the right path, Koontz was on track for an ordinary life. His childhood, as he has shared publicly, was marked by abuse and fear, with a father who harbored a homicidal fixation on him. He was protected by a strong mother and married a strong, loving woman. Despite his early trauma, it's easy to see that he has overcome that self-reported horrible childhood and grown into a grounded, generous, and prolific, highly successful, self-actualized adult.

In today's digital world, Koontz receives more than 20,000 fan letters a year—and reads every one. Those he chooses to respond to receive a handwritten letter from him, like the excerpt shown above.

This simple act says much about his values and his integration of self. He has not lost his humanity despite massive success—perhaps one of the strongest markers of self-actualization.

260

Lesson Twenty-Five
The Big Five

The "Big Five-factor" model is a widely accepted theory of personality and can be applied to handwriting fairly easily. It has been around since the 1980s. If you want to know the background, a quick Google search for "Big Five personality dimensions" will yield millions of results.

For our purposes, we'll focus on identifying these traits and how they are expressed in handwriting. A 2016 article in *Business Insider* applies the Big Five to leadership roles. Some key takeaways:

- ***Conscientiousness*** *is the strongest predictor of leadership*
- ***Extroversion*** *is also a strong predictor of who will become a leader, although introverts can succeed in leadership as well.*
- ***Agreeable*** *people tend to be happier, while disagreeable people may be more successful at work—possibly because they get their ideas forward more forcefully.*

As with most personality measures, the Big Five traits exist along a continuum. They are said to remain relatively stable across the lifespan, with research that suggests a genetic influence. Heritability estimates are at around 50%.

The acronym **OCEAN** makes them easy to remember:

— *Openness to experience*

— *Conscientiousness*

— *Extroversion*

— *Agreeableness*

— *Neuroticism*

261

Each of the following pairs describes the opposite ends of the continuum. Most people fall somewhere in between.

1. Openness to Experience

Preference for routine, practical ←—→ *imaginative, spontaneous*

Handwriting:

- ○ **Low openness**: *tends toward the conventional, copybook, strong regularity, organized, some left trend, arcade forms, narrow left margin*

- ○ **High openness**: *originality, simplification, released rhythm, airy spatial arrangement, garland forms, right trend.*

2. Conscientiousness

Impulsive, disorganized ←—→ *disciplined, careful*

Handwriting:

- ○ **Low conscientiousness**: *poor spatial arrangement, lack of organization, irregularity, (wavy baseline, changing slant, size)*

- ○ **High conscientiousness**: *good spatial arrangement, balanced, carefully placed i-dots, t-bars, strong regularity.*

3. Extroversion

Reserved, thoughtful ←—→ *sociable, fun-loving*

Handwriting:

- ○ **Introverted**: *smaller size, narrowness, emphasis on upper zone, secondary expansion, wider word spaces, tighter rhythm*

- ○ **Extroverted**: *larger overall size, rightward trend, looser rhythm, some primary thread, narrower overall spatial arrangement.*

4. Agreeableness

Calm, confident ←—→ *anxious, pessimistic*

Handwriting:

- ○ **Low agreeableness**: *extreme pressure (heavy or light), cramped spatial arrangement, narrow letters, falling baseline.*

- ○ *High agreeableness: medium pressure, mixed/balanced forms, balanced rhythm, strong capital letters, steady baseline (or slightly rising baseline)*

5. Neuroticism

Suspicious, uncooperative ⟷ trusting, helpful

Handwriting:

- ○ ***High neuroticism****: narrow and cramped, linear, angle forms, wide right margin, tall stroke on 'p'*

- ○ ***Low neuroticism****: mixed forms with some thread, narrower right margin, open spatial arrangement, open letters, slightly rising baseline.*

263

Lesson Twenty-Six
Other Needs

While Maslow's hierarchy provides a widely accepted framework for understanding human motivation, it does not account for every driving force. Some motivators fall outside the five classic levels—or may be seen as extreme expressions of them. One such powerful motivator is the need for power itself.

The Need for Power

— *Strength or force exerted or capable of being exerted*

— *Forcefulness; effectiveness*

An excellent example of this need is found in the handwriting of former General Electric CEO Jack Welch, introduced earlier in the course and seen on the following page. His script displays:

- *Dynamic movement*

- *Apparently strong pressure (we don't have an original to examine)*

- *An overall forceful appearance*

These features signal someone who refuses to take a back seat. Welch's handwriting radiates assertiveness. He is not just ambitious, he must be out front, leading the charge. That doesn't mean he's popular or nice, however.

It's important to distinguish this from the person operating at a lower motivational level who seeks money as a buffer against insecurity. Although power and money seem to go together, the power-driven personality values money not for safety or comfort, but as a means to acquire greater influence, authority, and control. Financial gain is a tool, not a destination.

265

Jack Welch

everything --- Your year at Medical, your selection as CEO of the best Company in the world and the wonderful start you have in this new role. I knew you were really good ---- but you are even better than I could imagine.

Congratulations on the $_____ --- it is just the beginning!

I look forward to cheering you on and will always be available when you feel it would be useful.

Another example of power motivation can be found in the handwriting of former Texas governor Ann Richards.

Although her handwriting follows a copybook style, especially in the capital letters—which is technically a weak form—what elevates it is the movement.

This is a dynamic and forward-driving handwriting, leaving little doubt about her need to lead. The copybook form notwithstanding, her script projects strength and assertiveness, much like the woman herself.

The space is weak (crowded), but with large, forceful handwriting like this, the fact that it was written on a postcard may well have impacted the arrangement. Only by analyzing additional samples written on a full-size page would we know whether this was her normal spatial style.

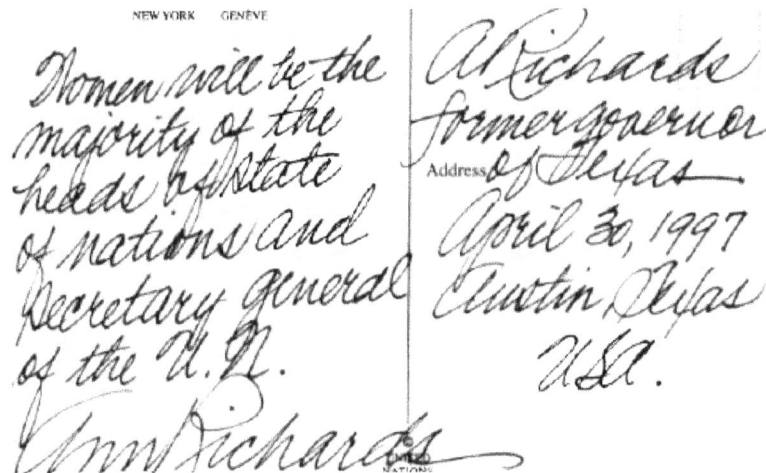

The Need to Create

Characterized by originality and expressiveness

Creativity is often seen as part of the self-actualization level, but in many ways it goes beyond it. The urge to create—genuinely and originally—is a powerful inner drive that can define a person's entire life.

There are many classical painters who faithfully render beautiful, realistic images of flowers or fruit with photographic accuracy. But that type of precision-based skill is not what we're talking about. While many forms of creativity exist, true expressive creativity as we are considering it is less about replication and more about exploration and transformation. Our focus is on that which departs from convention, where form is subordinated to inspiration; where imagination overrides structure, and something wholly new emerges.

General Handwriting Indicators of Expressive Creativity

In such writers, the handwriting is often:

- *Simplified*
- *Originality in overall form*
- *Combined connective forms, with a slight emphasis on thread.*
- *Spatially airy and open, reflecting mental freedom*
- *Smooth breaks in the writing line, symbolizing fluid thought and imagination.*

267

These characteristics gives the writer freedom of movement on the page, just as their mind moves freely across the boundaries of conventional thinking.

An interesting example is the handwriting of Jackson Pollock, the abstract expressionist, Jackson Pollock, known for his "drip and splash" paintings. Pollock said:

"On the floor I am more at ease, I feel nearer, more a part of the painting, since this way I can walk around in it, work from the four sides and be literally `in' the painting."

Pollock's handwriting reflects this same immersive freedom:

- *It is simplified and original*
- *Warm, pastose strokes*
- *The form, while informal, remains expressive and self-assured*

Understanding what motivates the writer, and identifying the level of need they are operating from, makes you better equipped to accurately answer a wide range of questions about personality. Whether the drive is for safety, affection, esteem, power, or originality, each leaves its mark on the page.

Lesson Twenty-Seven
The Dominant Picture

More important than assigning one-to-one meanings ("this means that") is understanding how the graphic indicators relate to one other in the specific handwriting you are analyzing. As you've heard throughout this course, context is everything. Once again:

No single feature has absolute meaning apart from its place within the overall structure of the writing.

Let's now review some of the basic concepts we have covered.

- *The spatial arrangement on the page represents how the writer views the world around him (superego) and how he organizes his life.*

- *The form or style of writing represents how the writer sees himself within his world (ego) and how he interacts with others.*

- *The movement of the writing on the paper represents how the writer behaves within his world (id).*

With these concepts in mind, the next step is to determine which of the three big pictures—space, form, or movement is dominant.

How to Determine the Dominant Picture

Hold the handwriting sample at a short distance, as if you were viewing a painting. Look at the whole—do not zoom in on isolated traits just yet.

If you find yourself mentally dissecting small parts of the writing, try flipping the page upside down. This helps shift your frame of reference and allows your brain to take in the total visual impression.

Ask yourself:

- *Is this person well balanced overall?*

- *What kind of person might this be?*

Interpreting Dominance and Disturbance

- *If something jumps out visually, there may be an imbalance in that area of functioning.*

- *If nothing does stand out, and the writing feels harmonious and whole, the sample likely has a good gestalt—a sign of internal balance and integration.*

Examples of Disturbance:

Too much dark space (overcrowding), indicates disturbed spatial arrangement. This suggests issues with perspective, boundaries, or clear thinking—Space is dominant but poorly balanced.

Excessive white space reflects the opposite extreme—over-isolation or emotional distance—again, space is dominant but poorly balanced.

Writing that seems chaotic, with too much variation in size, slant, or margins, points to disturbed movement. This suggests problems on a very basic level of functioning and self-discipline—impulsivity, instability, or poor self-discipline. Movement is dominant.

Elaborate or overly ornamental forms often reveal issues with self-image or affectation—problems with the ego—Form is dominant.

In many cases, more than one of the big pictures may be weak or disturbed. When this occurs, it indicates multi-dimensional difficulties in emotional, intellectual, or behavioral functioning.

When form and/or movement are disturbed by the spatial arrangement is clear, according to Felix Klein, the writer can still function well in the world.

A Good Gestalt in Practice

Let's look at the handwriting of one of the early classical graphologists, Dr. Hans Knobloch. When you first glance at this sample, what stands out? *Nothing*—and that's the point. The writing appears balanced, well-composed, and harmonious. Nothing looks out of place. No single element pulls your attention more than another.

The writing doesn't beg for correction. It feels complete.

This is the very definition of a good gestalt.

Exercise

Describe this handwriting sample of Dr. Hans Knobloch in terms of its:

— *Spatial arrangement*

— *Writing form*

— *Movement.*

At this stage, your task is simply to describe the handwriting—*what you see, not what it means.*

After you have completed your examination, write one paragraph describing what the handwriting implies in terms of personality functioning. Then, check your observations against the following analysis.

271

Now Take a Closer Look: What Gives This Writing a Good Gestalt?

Space:

The spatial arrangement is strong—clean and organized. The margins are clear and balanced. Word spacing is slightly wide (typical of European handwriting), but still harmonious. Line spacing is also broad, but accommodates the lower zone length, maintaining balance.

Form:

The writing form is strong due to its positive simplification. The writer has moved beyond copybook without compromising legibility. There are no extra loops, flourishes, no beginning or ending strokes. The writing is stripped to essentials without losing legibility, conveying clarity and purpose.

Movement:

The movement is strong with a dynamic rightward trend. It shows energy without aggression. While pressure cannot be measured directly from a photocopy, we can observe the rhythmic alternation of light/dark in the up/down-strokes, suggesting suggests an even and forceful flow of ink—a sign of emotional continuity and vitality.

Conclusion (First Impression)

This writer displays self-confidence, energy, and the stamina follow through on tasks. He values efficiency and prefers to cut to the chase. Routine details make him impatient; his focus is on the big picture, not the minutiae.

Now that you've sketched a basic personality profile from your initial view of the gestalt, let's go deeper.

Advanced Exercise

Use the handwriting sample to identify which elements of his handwriting support the following personality conclusions about Dr. Knobloch. For each one, ask: What features support this?

272

1. Social Attitude

Although he is basically a 'feeling' person, that layer is hidden under an intellectual outlook. He sees the world objectively and does not suffer fools gladly. His communication style is direct and precise, saying exactly what he thinks, though not unkindly. He values diplomacy, but may grow impatient if others takes too long to explain themselves.

2. Cognitive/Intellectual functioning:

He is interested in philosophical and abstract ideas, with no desire for small talk. A visionary thinker, he uses intuition to pick up environmental cues. His "mental antenna" is tuned in to what is going on around him, selecting relevant information and applying it meaningfully and at the right moment.

3. Ego Strength

His ego is well-developed—quietly confident and self-directing. He has no need to boast. His behavior is generally appropriate to the situation. He is capable of delaying gratification, acting with maturity and purpose.

4. Drives and Motivation

He is driven by the need to produce, to generate new ideas, and to be intellectually creative. His best work would be in partnership with someone who can manage routine tasks, freeing him from the humdrum, routine to pursue high-level conceptual aims.

Final Step: Test the Profile Against the Indicators

Go back to your observations of:

— *Margins*
— *Letter, word, and line spacing*
— *Baseline behavior.*

Then ask yourself:

Do these meanings align with the strength of the spatial arrangement and form?' If the answer is yes, the interpretations are likely valid and will contribute to understanding Dr. Knobloch's core issues and overall functioning.

Another Example: Disturbed Gestalt

At a glance, something is clearly off. The gestalt is seriously disturbed—you immediately sense that something needs to be "fixed." But what's the problem?

Before reading further, take a moment to describe the handwriting in terms of its three "big pictures:"

— *Space*

— *Form*

— *Movement*

Then write a short paragraph interpreting what these qualities may reveal about the writer's personality functioning.

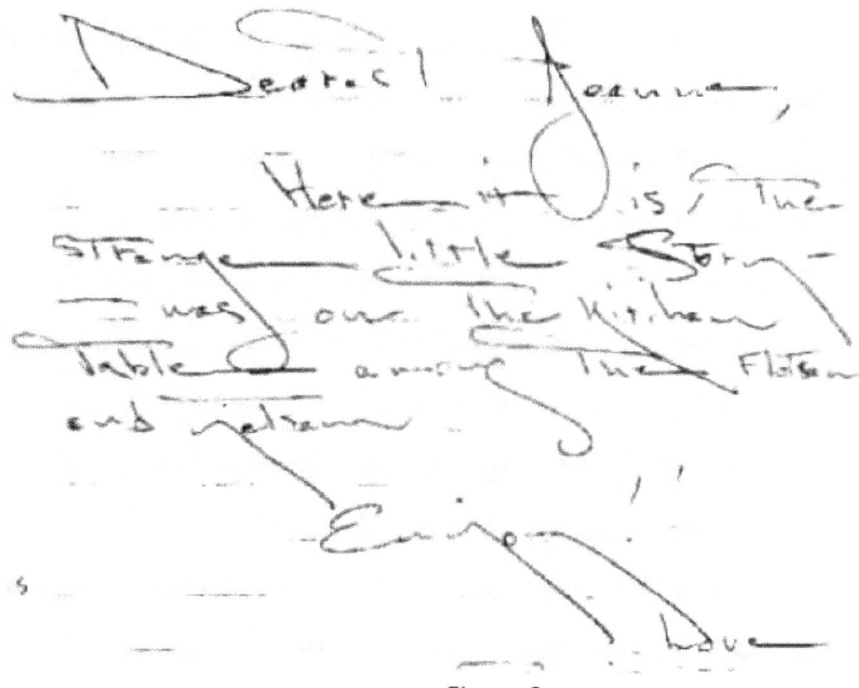

Background

The writer is a woman in her 70's.

Space: The spatial arrangement is disturbed, due to extreme lower zone intrusions that disrupt the balance of the page.

274

Form: The writing form is also disturbed. The script switches inconsistently between cursive and printing, showing no integration between styles.

Movement: The movement is disturbed, with shifting slants, and a lower zone that veers in the wrong direction, indicating instability and erratic emotional expression.

In this example, all three big pictures—space, form, and movement are disturbed. This demonstrates serious disruptions in psychological functioning.

The writer has been diagnosed with Bipolar Disorder, which, assuming she was in a state of "high" at the time of writing, helps explain the wild, uncontrolled nature of the movement.

Important Reminder: Unless you are a licensed clinician, do not diagnose a mental or physical illness based solely on handwriting. Your role is to describe observable behaviors, not to assign medical labels.

That said, understanding the behavioral patterns found in personality and anxiety disorders is important for graphologists. For more on this topic, see my book co-authored with the late psychologist and graphologist Dr. Ze'ev Bar-Av, which addresses abnormal personality and handwriting.

Bipolar Disorder

Bipolar Personality Disorder (formerly manic-depressive illness) causes dramatic mood swings between manic and depressive states.

- *In the manic phase, behaviors may include rapid speech, racing thoughts, impulsivity, grandiosity, sexual over-activity, irritability, and a refusal to admit anything is wrong.*

- *In the depressive phase, the individual may feel hopeless, fatigued, anxious, and may withdraw entirely. Sleep is disrupted. Pleasure and motivation disappear. Suicidal ideation may occur.*

These emotional shifts appear directly in handwriting, but the same writer may display very different script characteristics depending on the phase of illness at the time of writing.

In the sample above, the handwriting shows diffuse, uncontrolled energy. You might imagine her speaking faster than her thoughts can keep up. The rhythm is erratic, the structure is weak, and there is an intense need to be seen—while paradoxically pushing others away.

Example #3

Next is an example of a disturbed movement pattern—an "id" writing in Gestalt terms.

Contrast Example: Moderately Balanced and Active

This sample is from a 39-year-old man in practice as a business coach.

- *The writing shows a slight emphasis on movement, indicating energy and dynamism. The rhythm is a little on the slack side.*

- *Pressure is good, suggesting stamina.*

- *The writer enjoys physical activity (e.g., baseball) and rarely sits still.*

- *He is enthusiastic and fully committed to his clients.*

- *The form is a simplified version of copybook—clear, functional, and consistent.*

- *The spatial arrangement is balanced and well-organized.*

- *This is a strong example of someone operating from healthy ego strength, grounded in purposeful, energetic action.*

Final Exercise

Now it's your turn.

Using the samples that follow this section, apply everything you've learned. You don't need to turn in these exercises unless you have specific questions, but practice is essential for your development as a graphologist.

Instructions

1. View the handwriting as a whole. Turn it upside down if you need to shift your frame of reference.

2. Ask yourself: Does anything stand out? If so, which of the three big pictures—space, form, or movement, does it belong to?

3. Describe each of the big pictures. Identify which is strongest, weakest, or possibly disturbed. Or are all balanced?

4. Write a short paragraph describing each big picture. Focus strictly on description, not interpretation—at first.

5. Now, interpret your findings. Based on the gestalt, write a short personality sketch. If you have studied up on the Enneagram or another typology, see if you can figure out the writer's type.

In Closing

Now that you know the basic principles of Gestalt graphology, here comes the hard part:

Practice, practice, practice.

It takes time to "get it" — just like learning to read. You began by sounding out one word at a time. Then, one day, you could read full sentences without thinking about how you did it.

That moment will come, too.

One day, you'll pick up a handwriting sample and know what it says—before you even put it into words.

Until then, stay curious. Stay observant. And enjoy the process.

Meanwhile, one last important word...

Compassionate Interpretation

As a handwriting analyst, it's important to balance realism with encouragement. When analyzing handwriting, especially that of struggling individuals, remember: the signs of that struggle may be evident, but don't just look for what's wrong and overwhelm the client with a list of deficits—*look for what's working*. Even in difficult samples, you can find compensatory traits—evidence of the writer's coping mechanisms, their resourcefulness or resilience. Focus on identifying those inner strengths–the *coping mechanisms* in their writing—and frame your interpretation and suggestions in a way that supports growth may be beneficial. Remember:

Don't just look for what's wrong. Look for what's working.

You are always welcome to contact me with questions or comments. Enjoy your journey!

—Sheila Lowe

Practice Samples

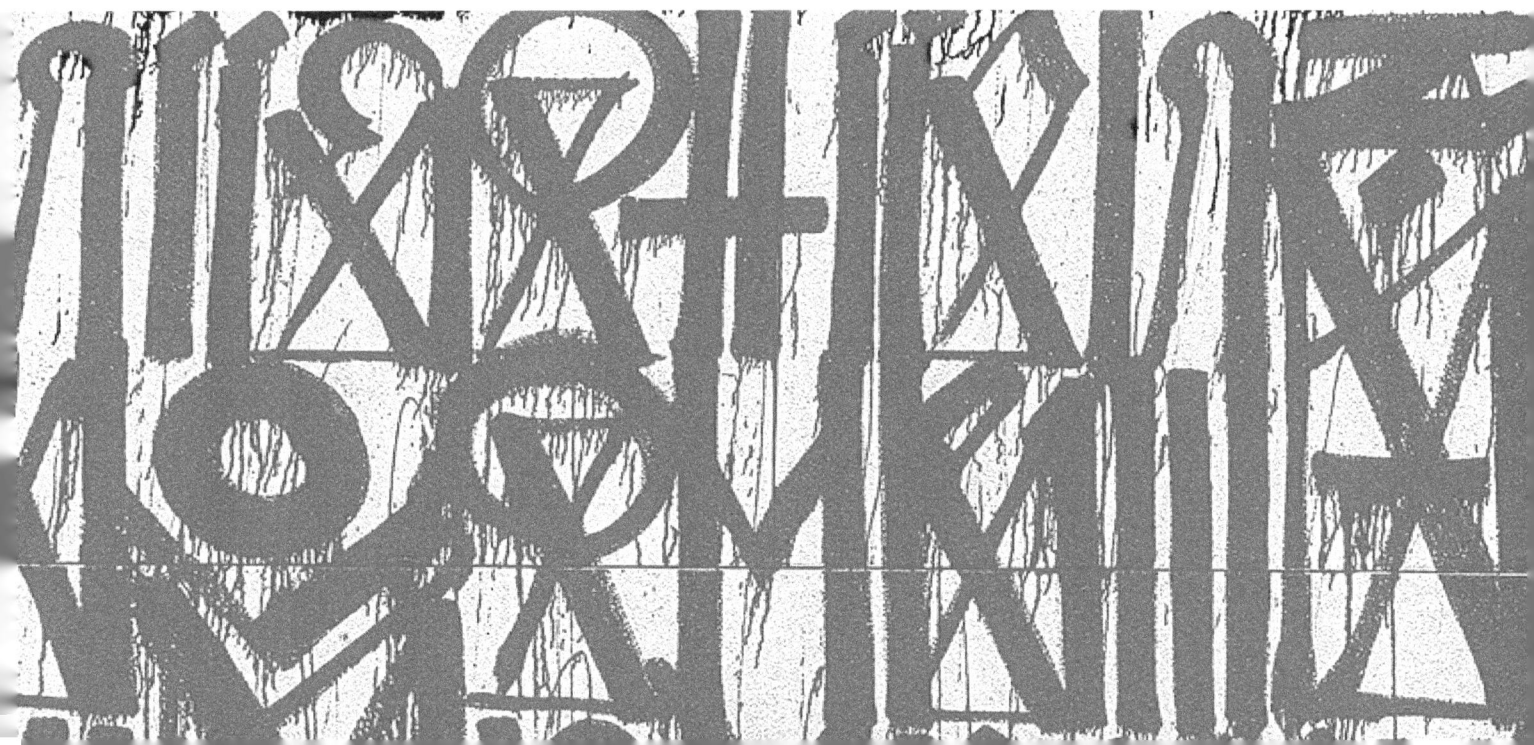

Male, late 40s - how open-minded is this person? Is he willing to explore new ideas, or does he stick with what he knows?

1. What are the characteristics of a good/trusted friend?

For me, a good and trusted friend is someone who exhibits such characteristics as honesty, integrity, and forthrightness, yet is willing to criticize or say what needs to be said to me — in other words, constructive criticism for helpful purposes. A trusted friend is not a sycophant, nor hypercritical or controlling; the key phrase is firm but fair.

ENCLOSED IS A LETTER WRITTEN BY A
PROFESSIONAL CON-ARTIST, LIER, CHEAT
AND LESBIAN.

MY CLIENT HIRED HER TO TAKE CARE
OF HER 91 YR. OLD FATHER. WITH IN 6
MONTHS THIS WOMAN RAN UP #4,000 IN
CREDIT CARD CHARGES WHICH SHE FORGED
UNDER THE 91 YR OLD MAN'S NAME. SHE
ALSO HAD HER GIRLFRIEND MOVE IN AND
HAD TWO GUNS IN THE HOUSE; A .38 CAL
HAND GUN AND AN "OOZI"!

I HAD THEM EVICTED WITH THE HELP
OF THE POLICE. THEY THEN FORWARDED
THE OLD MANS MAIL TO THERE NEW ADD-
RESS. THERE IS A STRONG POSSIBILITY THAT
THEY DRUGGED MY CLIENT'S FATHER. HE
IS NOW IN BED AND MAY BE DYING.
THEY WROTE MY CLIENT THIS LETTER
AFTER THEY WERE EVICTED. NOTICE THE
POSTMARK IS HONOLULU. I BELIEVE SHE
IS STILL HERE IN LAKEWOOD CALIF WHERE HER
MAIL HAS BEEN FORWARDED. THOUGHT YOU
WOULD ENJOY THE WRITING FOR YOUR FILES!

Female, middle-aged

3-16 T/C TO OWNER-She will take
Vehicle into shop ASAP-
I advised - she take our estimate
To shop with her.

3-17 11AM I Spoke w/Shop DAVE excepted
our repair cost. - No Supplements -
or Vehicle will be TOTAl Loss.
DAVE understands our position.
I'll close this file by the 20TH.

Female, 30s

I am puzzled. I used to be angry
all the time just like him then
I decided one day that I was
tired. Tired of everything always
in pain, afraid of living happy.
So I stopped. I opened my
eyes one day and made a
conscious decision that no more
will my emotions control me.
I am in control! I will
live my life happier and not
be afraid anymore.

Peace & Love

Male, 47

in Atlantic City, NJ in 1951.
I grew up on a Chicken & Egg Farm. I was one of the few Jewish kids in a German-Catholic neighborhood. My father died when I was 15. I went to a small liberal arts college in central Pa called Juniata College. I went to graduate school at Temple University. After graduate school I moved to New York and have lived here for over twenty years. I have gradually moved up the corporate ladder and moved toward entertainment, which is where I feel I have the best fit. I now am concentrating on completing and fulfilling my

2. What kind of person are you interested in or looking for: personal life desires.

2/1/99

?etheart,

How's mom's Biggest man? I PRAY FOR you AND US everynight. I miss you so much I Love you to Pieces. I Love you! I Love yo I Love you! I miss us Being together as one so much;"It hurts". I CAN't WAit to hug you, and squeeze you, Kiss you, PLAyLeg AND CHRS with you. Your mom's #1! your the Best! PLEASE Be moms Biggest MAN AND show them how you CAN go Poty By yourself. You CAN Do it! You've Done it FOR me. "Go BRucey Go! God Bless you.

I LOVE you
LOVE, mommy

Female, late 30s

THANK YOU SO VERY MUCH FOR
REMAINING ON THE UCPWN BOARD FOR
YET ANOTHER YEAR. SINCE I'VE BEEN
ON THE BOARD WITH YOU, WE'VE BEEN
TRYING TO ATTRACT YOUNGER WOMEN,
AND NOW WE'VE GOT SOME ON THE
BOARD! YOU, SHIRLEY, AND I WILL
NEED TO GUIDE THEM AS THEY, HOPE-
FULLY, BRING NEW IDEAS THAT WILL
ATTRACT EVEN MORE NEW MEMBERS—
OF ALL AGES!

THANKS AGAIN,

RECOMMENDED READING

GRAPHOLOGY

Lazewnik, Baruch - *Handwriting Analysis, a Guide to Understanding Personalities*; Whitford Press, W. Chester, PA; 1990

Lowe, Sheila R. - *Reading Between the Lines: Decoding Handwriting;* Write Choice Ink, 2018

Lowe, Sheila R. - *Advanced Studies in Handwriting Psychology*; Write Choice Ink, 2025

Bar-Av Zeev, Sheila R. Lowe - *Personality and Anxiety Disorders, Collected Works of;* Write Choice Ink, 2018

Farmer, Jeanette - *Personality and Anxiety Disorders, Collected Works of;* Write Choice Ink, 2025

Griffiths, Renate - *Personality and Anxiety Disorders, Collected Works of;* Write Choice Ink, 2025

Henley, Terry, June Canoles, Renate Griffiths - *Personality and Anxiety Disorders, Collected Works of;* Write Choice Ink, 2025

Mendel, Alfred O. - *Personality in Handwriting;* Newcastle Books, Van Nuys, CA; 1990

Nezos, Renna - *Graphology, the Interpretation of Handwriting*; Trafalgar Square/David & Charles, N. Pomfret, VT; 1986

Olyanova, Nadya - *Handwriting Tells*; Bell Publishing Company, New York, NY;

Pulver, Max - *Symbolism of Handwriting*; Scriptor Books, London, England; 1994

Roman, Klara - *Handwriting, a Key to Personality*; Pantheon Books; New York, NY; 1975

Rubin, Roger - *Personality and Anxiety Disorders, Collected Works of;* Write Choice Ink, 2025;

Seifer, Marc - *The Definitive Book of Handwriting Analysis*; Weiser; 2008

Teillard, Ana - *The Soul in Handwriting*; Scriptor Books; London, England, 1995

Victor, Frank - *Handwriting, a Personality Projection;* Fern Ridge Press, Eugene, OR; 1989

Hartford, Huntington - *You Are What You Write*; Macmillan Pub. Co., New York, NY; 1973

Sonnemann, Ulrich - *Handwriting Analysis*; Grune & Stratton, New York, NY; 1950

Various authors; edited by Sheila Lowe - *The Power of the Pen: From the unconscious to the conscious* - An Anthology, Write Choice Ink 2022

Some out of print books may be available through eBay and https://mostlybooksaz.com/

Members of the American Handwriting Analysis Foundation may find these and thousands of other resources in the AHAF Library.

PSYCHOLOGY

American Psychiatric Association: *Diagnostic & Statistical Manual of Mental Disorders*, Fifth Edition; Washington, D.C. ("DSM V"), 2022

Ewen, Robert B.; *Introduction to Theories of Personality* Fourth Edition, Lawrence Erlbaum, Associates, Publishers, 1993

Current texts on Introductory Psychology; Abnormal Psychology; Developmental Psychology

Arnheim, Rudolf; *Art and Visual Perception, a Psychology of the Creative Eye,* The New Version, University of California Press, Berkeley and Los Angeles, CA 1974

(Texts may be obtained from a local university or library, or Lawrence Erlbaum, Publishers)

GENERAL SUBJECT INDEX

Movement, Rhythm, Zones

P

People

Pressure

293

EXPERIMENTAL INDEX

Generated by Chat GPT

297

138, 147, 149, 156, 157, 158, 159, 162, 163, 164, 222, 279

Wide: 4, 29, 32, 38, 39, 41, 42, 45, 46, 48, 51, 52, 53, 57, 58, 59, 65, 66, 97, 98, 100, 106, 115, 120, 159, 162, 174, 177, 180, 182, 187, 190, 192, 194, 203, 213, 225, 230, 250, 281

Widening: 55

Wolfgang Kohler: 11

psychology: 7, 11, 12, 14, 15, 16, 23, 98, 106, 202, 299

"Eye" training: 183, 217

About the Author

Sheila Lowe is a forensic handwriting examiner, author, and educator with over fifty years of experience decoding the written word. Her nonfiction books include Reading Between the Lines: Handwriting Decoded and her memoir, Growing From the Ashes. In the best-selling Forensic Handwriting suspense series, Sheila's real-world expertise drives unforgettable fiction as she bridges science and mystery with every stroke of the pen. Her Beyond the Veil paranormal suspense series features a woman who talks to dead people.

www.sheilalowe.com

www.sheilalowebooks.com

facebook.com/SheilaLoweBooks
twitter.com/Sheila_Lowe
instagram.com/SheilaLoweBooks
bookbub.com/authors/sheila-lowe
goodreads.com/sheilalowe
linkedin.com/in/sheilalowe

Also By Sheila Lowe

NONFICTION

Reading Between the Lines: Decoding Handwriting

Advanced Studies in Handwriting Psychology

Personality & Anxiety Disorders

Succeeding in the Business of Handwriting Analysis

Improve Your Life with Graphotherapy

Sheila Lowe's Handwriting Analyzer software

Handwriting of the Famous & Infamous

The Complete Idiot's Guide to Handwriting Analysis

FORENSIC HANDWRITING SERIES

Poison Pen

Written In Blood

Dead Write

Last Writes

Inkslingers Ball

Outside The Lines

Written Off

Dead Letters

Maximum Pressure

BEYOND THE VEIL SERIES

What She Saw

Proof of Life

The Last Door

www.ingramcontent.com/pod-product-compliance
Lightning Source LLC
Chambersburg PA
CBHW080130270326
41926CB00021B/4421